BRITISH WRITERS AND THEIR WORK: NO. 6

General Editors
Bonamy Dobrée and T. O. Beachcroft

Editor of the American Edition
J. W. Robinson

SAMUEL RICHARDSON

by R. F. Brissenden

HENRY FIELDING

by John Butt

LAURENCE STERNE

by D. W. Jefferson

TOBIAS SMOLLETT

by Laurence Brander

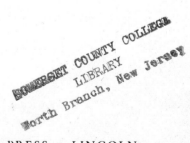
UNIVERSITY OF NEBRASKA PRESS • LINCOLN

Samuel Richardson by R. F. Brissenden, *Henry Fielding* by John Butt, *Laurence Sterne* by D. W. Jefferson, and *Tobias Smollett* by Laurence Brander originally appeared separately in pamphlet form, published by Longmans, Green & Co. for The British Council and the National Book League [of Great Britain]. The Bison Book edition is published by arrangement with The British Council.

Manufactured in the United States of America

PREFACE

BRITISH WRITERS AND THEIR WORK is addressed to the student who wants a general introduction to a particular writer or group of writers, and also to the more advanced student and to the lover of literature who enjoy fresh, thoughtful literary criticism. Each volume includes essays on from two to six writers, the series as a whole being planned to consider British men of letters from the fourteenth century to the present day. The essays in most instances combine the biography of a writer with a critical appreciation of his work. Many of the contributors are themselves well-known English authors and critics.

The essays originally were published separately for The British Council under the titles listed on the copyright page. They are reprinted in the American edition with minor corrections.

It is hoped that not only will the essays prove useful and stimulating, but that the select bibliographies will make each volume a convenient, portable reference work. While the arrangement will vary somewhat from volume to volume, each essay usually is followed by a full list of the first editions of the writer's works (provided as a complement to the account in the essay); a list of collected editions, modern reprints, and student editions; a list of bibliographies and reference works; and a list of critical and biographical studies (including both standard works and other works found especially useful by the author of the essay). Each volume ordinarily concludes with a list of general works. The select bibliographies are based largely on the bibliographies originally published with the essays.

J. W. R.

CONTENTS

I

SAMUEL RICHARDSON

by R. F. Brissenden

Mr. S. Richardson.

C. Grignion sculp.

SAMUEL RICHARDSON

From the engraved frontispiece to the first volume of Rivington's 7 vol.
edition of *Sir Charles Grandison*, 1766.

Samuel Richardson was born in Derbyshire in 1689. He died on July 4, 1761, in London and was buried at St. Bride's, Fleet Street.

SAMUEL RICHARDSON

I

Few genuinely great novelists have been so extravagantly praised in their own day and so thoroughly neglected by succeeding generations as Samuel Richardson. During the eighteenth century he was probably more famous and more influential than any other novelist in Europe. His three novels, *Pamela*, *Clarissa* and *Sir Charles Grandison* were translated into all the major European languages; they were read by people in every rank of society; and in some countries—notably France, Germany and England itself—they had a profound effect on the development of the novel. In a famous pronouncement after Richardson's death in 1761, Denis Diderot, one of the major literary and intellectual figures of the age, declared that he was fit company for the immortals, and that his works merited a place on the same shelf as those of Moses, Homer, Sophocles and Euripides. Yet not much more than a hundred years later an English scholar was able to dismiss Richardson confidently with the remark that he was typical of 'that class of writers who are . . . read by none but the critic, the connoisseur or the historian of literature'.

In recent years the critical estimate of his novels has begun to rise again, but there are still many who would claim that Richardson's importance today is mainly historical. It is understandable that this should be so, for his faults, both as a novelist and as a man, are obvious and unpleasant. To begin with, the sheer size of his novels is enough to daunt the reader: he takes almost a million words to tell the story of *Sir Charles Grandison*, and *Clarissa* is even longer. But his 'insupportable prolixity', as an eighteenth century critic calls it, is not nearly so objectionable as the vein of prurience, hypocrisy and sheer vulgarity, which, in varying degrees, runs through everything he ever wrote. In *Clarissa* and to a certain extent in *Sir Charles Grandison* this merges more or less completely into the general pattern of the work; but in *Pamela*, his first novel, its effect is extremely damaging: the structure of the whole book is seriously distorted.

Pamela is the story of a young, beautiful and intelligent maidservant who staves off seduction so skilfully that she is able to convince her wicked master that he ought to reform and marry her. Unfortunately Pamela's virtue is not quite so innocent as Richardson intended it to be. The world is not likely to forget this easily: it is a commonplace of literary history that, despite or perhaps because of its extraordinary popularity, this novel inspired several parodies including the aptly titled and amusing *Shamela*, and the opening chapters of *Joseph Andrews*. But it is a mistake to condemn *Clarissa* or even *Sir Charles Grandison* because of the notorious weaknesses of their elder sister. Even Henry Fielding, who was almost certainly the author of *Shamela* as well as of *Joseph Andrews*, paid unqualified tribute to *Clarissa*. 'Such Simplicity, such Manners, such deep Penetration into Nature; such Power to raise and alarm the Passions few Writers, either ancient or modern, have been possessed of,' he stated in his periodical, *The Jacobite's Journal*; and in a personal letter to the author which has only recently come to light, he speaks with an even more generous enthusiasm of Richardson's powers as a writer, and freely admits that the sufferings of his heroine have moved him to tears. The letter is typical of the warmth and honesty of Fielding's character. Richardson's response was typical too: when *Tom Jones* appeared its success piqued his vanity, and he lost no time in abusing this 'truly coarse-titled' book and its 'low' and immoral author, in private letters to his friends.

Yet Fielding's praise of *Clarissa* is entirely justified: in many ways it is the greatest novel of its day. It has defects it is true: it is over long, it is written in an epistolary convention which, especially to the modern reader, seems artificial and awkward, and it is pervaded with an air of moral solemnity which becomes at times oppressive. But the book has a naked realism, a moral and pyschological insight, and a sustained and compelling dramatic force which set it above most of the other works of fiction produced in the eighteenth century. Narrow as Richardson's range may be, in *Clarissa* he strikes deeper into the heart of his own age than either of his two great contemporaries, Sterne and Fielding, ever do. One reason for this, perhaps, is that he strikes deeper into his own heart than do most novelists. It is painfully clear that he is to an unusual extent personally involved in the problems about which he is writing. As a result there is an air of urgency and suspense to his work which is lacking in *Tom Jones* or *Tristram Shandy*. *Clarissa*, in particular, once one has become immersed in the story, has an almost hypnotic effect: it is a book which in a quite unrelenting fashion engages both the heart and the mind to the full. Not only is it a work of considerable moral significance but also, despite its length, it is extremely readable.

Pamela and *Sir Charles Grandison* are important books, and *Clarissa* is a great one. Yet it is impossible to regard Richardson himself as a great man. That this timid, sanctimonious, prudish business man should somehow have been able to create the sombre and powerful tragedy of *Clarissa* is one of those embarrassing paradoxes with which history occasionally presents us. The character of Richardson is an affront to every conception of what an artist should be: and indeed there can be no doubt that he was to a large extent an artist by accident and despite himself. When, as he put it himself, he 'slid into the writing of *Pamela*,' he was, to all outward appearances, nothing but a middle-aged London printer, respected and prosperous, but in no way distinguished. He was then fifty-one years old, having been born in 1689, and in his career up to this point he had not deviated in the slightest from the conventional middle-class pattern of material advancement through virtue and hard work. It was not without pride that, in later life, he described his apprenticeship:

I served a diligent Seven years to it, to a Master who grudged every Hour to me, that tended not to his Profit, even of those Times of Leisure & Diversion, which the Refractoriness of my Fellow Servants *obliged* him to allow them, and were usually allowed by other Masters to their Apprentices. I stole from the Hours of Rest & Relaxation, my Reading Times for Improvement of my Mind ... But ... I took Care, that even my Candle was of my own purchasing, that I might not in the most trifling Instance make my Master a Sufferer.

Like the virtuous apprentice in Hogarth's *Industry and Idleness* he married his master's daughter, and when she died he prudently took for his second wife the sister of an eminent bookseller in Bath. By the time he was fifty he had become an established figure in 'the trade' in London, with a flourishing business and a house on the rural outskirts of the city at 'agreeable suburbane North End'. He had also acquired the reputation of being a ready man with his pen, willing to oblige his fellow booksellers 'with writing Indexes, Prefaces, & sometimes for their minor Authors, *honest* Dedications; abstracting, abridging, compiling, and giving his Opinion of Pieces offered them'. Nobody, least of all Richardson himself, would ever have dreamed that he might one day have added the writing of novels to this list of sober and useful activities. Yet it was his colleagues' opinion of his literary abilities which indirectly led to his becoming a novelist.

In 1739 two booksellers, or publishers as they would now be called, asked him to compile for them a small volume of model letters for the use of people without much formal education or practice in correspondence. Such letter-writing manuals were not at all uncommon at this time, and in most respects Richardson's *Letters written to and for particular Friends*, or *Familiar Letters*, as it is more generally known, follows the conventional pattern fairly closely. Like all its fellows it would be quite forgotten today were it not that whilst he was writing it Richardson got the idea of using some of the model letters as the nucleus of a didactic

story. He had intended from the beginning that his manual
should not only teach people how to write letters but should
also be morally instructive; and in the course of composing
a group of letters designed to advise handsome servant girls
'how to avoid the Snares that might be laid against their
Virtue', he recalled a story he had once heard of one maidservant who had avoided the snares and won the hand of her
master into the bargain. In his own words, 'hence sprung
Pamela'.

II
'PAMELA'

There has perhaps never been a literary success quite like that of *Pamela*. Certainly no previous work of fiction had ever attained such rapid, widespread and enduring popularity, and few have since. *Pamela* seems to have appealed to every sort of potential reader, and although judged by modern standards the reading public at this time formed only a small proportion of the general population the book enjoyed a wide circulation. Fashionable ladies smiled at the heroine's 'lowness', but wept in their chambers over her trials; her virtue was praised in the pulpit; and, according to one story, the villagers at Slough rang the church bells to celebrate her marriage. Within a year *Pamela* had run through six impressions and had been translated into French. Translations into other languages soon followed; and it eventually became more popular on the Continent, where it inspired not only other novels but also several plays and an opera, than in England. *Pamela* became the archetypal Cinderella story of the age—in Lady Mary Wortley Montagu's phrase, 'the joy of the chambermaids of all nations'. Probably no other novel was read by so many people in the eighteenth century: in the general imagination of the period Pamela herself acquired something of the status of a mythical figure.

How are we to account for the extraordinary popularity of this novel? Part of the answer lies simply in its quality as a work of fiction: although the book as a whole may be justly criticized for its unevenness, its crudity, and its sentimentality, the first portion of the novel, that dealing with Mr. B.'s various attempts to seduce Pamela, is a lively and convincing piece of writing. Moreover the situation is presented with a psychological realism and a moral seriousness which were almost completely new in English fiction. These things would not have been enough in themselves, however: what guaranteed the success of *Pamela* was that in so many respects it was the right book at the right time. Since the end of the seventeenth century the demand for fiction had been growing steadily, largely as a result of an increase in the number of middle-class people, especially women, with enough leisure for reading. 'The world is so taken up of late with novels and romances, that it will be hard for a private history to be taken for genuine,' complained Defoe in 1722 in his preface to *Moll Flanders;* and in 1740, the year in which *Pamela* was published, there were enough works of fiction in print and enough people wanting to read them for the first circulating library in London to be opened. But mere quantity was not enough to satisfy this developing appetite: the majority of the 'novels and romances' published at this time were, as Richardson states on the title page of *Pamela*, 'Pieces calculated for Amusement only'. Whether they tended also to 'inflame the Minds they should instruct' is doubtful. Though their plots and titles are often erotic enough, the stories themselves are for the most part shallow, insipid and incredible. When something realistic, like Defoe's brilliant documentary narratives of contemporary life, was produced, it lacked psychological depth and subtlety.

Moreover, people wanted to be instructed as well as amused: it was their gentle didacticism as much as anything else which made *The Tatler* and *The Spectator* so popular; and even in this increasingly secular age books on religious subjects still constituted the largest single category of those published each year. Allegories like *The Pilgrim's Progress*, works of practical piety, such as *The Whole Duty of Man*, *Holy Living and Holy Dying*, and Defoe's various *Family Instructors* went through dozens of editions, and collections of sermons were best sellers. And the practicality of these and innumerable similar works was often as important as their piety: they were concerned with the most pressing social problems of the day—the status of women, the rearing of children, the extent to which private convictions should be allowed to conflict with social responsibilities. The author of *The Whole Duty of Man* spends more space discussing man's duty to his neighbours than in discussing his duty to God; and Defoe, in the dramatic dialogues in *Religious Courtship* is more concerned with problems of marriage than with problems of religion.

This is the tradition in which *Pamela*, like the *Familiar Letters*, was initially conceived. When Richardson began to write *Pamela* he probably had no intention of producing a novel at all. As the sub-title, *Virtue Rewarded*, indicates, his purpose was simply to use his story to demonstrate both that servant girls ought to resist the amorous advances of their masters and that Providence will look after them if they do. But in spite of his modest aim the conduct-book parable came alive in his hands and developed into a novel.

Richardson became a novelist primarily because he had the novelist's genius. But this genius needed something to release it. For Richardson this was effected through his intense concern with certain moral issues, a concern which was the result of a profound conflict within his own personality, a conflict between a strong and sympathetic sense of justice and an innate and almost pathological timidity. This conflict is reflected in all his writings: indeed it is out of the attempt to resolve it that his novels are born.

In the Preface to the *Familiar Letters* Richardson, speaking of himself in the third person, states that it has been his purpose through the letters

> to inculcate the Principles of *Virtue* and *Benevolence;* to describe *properly* and recommend *strongly*, the SOCIAL and RELATIVE DUTIES. . . .
>
> Particularly, he has endeavoured to point out the Duty of a *Servant* not a *Slave;* the Duty of a *Master* not a *Tyrant;* that of a *Parent,* not as a Person morose and sour, and hard to be pleased; but mild, indulgent, kind, and such a one as would rather govern by *Persuasion* than *Force.*

This could serve as an introduction to everything he ever wrote. The 'SOCIAL and RELATIVE DUTIES' are, in some form or other the theme of all his novels. He is preoccupied by the problem of the relation between the individual and the various social groups to which he belongs. What are the obligations which we owe to those who are socially either our superiors or our inferiors? What are the obligations which, in common humanity, we owe to others irrespective of class, sex, creed or nationality? And what are we to do when these two sets of duties come into conflict? Stated in the most general terms, these are the questions which Richardson continually raises and seeks to answer in his novels.

In some form or other these are the questions with which all serious novelists are concerned. Richardson is particularly interesting, however, because to begin with his attitude to these matters was not that of a novelist at all: he approached the whole problem of human conduct as a moral propagandist rather than an artist. But through the attempt to apply his dogmatic and relatively simple moral theory to the practical and untidy realities of life he developed, by a process of forced and often painful growth, not only into a novelist but also into a moral and social thinker of some force and profundity.

The process can be observed very clearly in *Pamela*. At the superficial level it is a tract on the virtues of chastity and, more particularly, dutifulness. The heroine succeeds in getting Mr. B. to marry her because no matter how sadistically he tries her she endeavours to treat him still with that respect to which as her master and as a man he is 'properly' entitled. The hypocritical twists and subterfuges through which Pamela goes—or is forced to go by Richardson—in order to keep up this façade of respect are amongst the more unpleasant and ridiculous features of the novel; and if Pamela's dutifulness were the only explanation for the eventual marriage of the hero and heroine the book would have been forgotten long ago. But the situation is more complex than it seems at first: Pamela finally gets her man not because she is dutiful to him, but because she succeeds in convincing him that he owes a duty to her, not

***

merely as a woman but simply as a human being. She does this by distinguishing with scrupulous thoroughness between the occasions on which he deserves to be respected and those on which he forfeits this right by trying to demand her obedience in an 'improper' way. After his attempt on her virtue in the summer-house, for instance, Pamela announces rebelliously that she won't stay:

> You won't, hussy! said he: Do you know whom you speak to? I lost all fear and all respect, and said, Yes, I do, Sir, too well!—well may I forget that I am your servant, when you forget what belongs to a master.

The scene is typical: every encounter between the two follows the same pattern of angry, passionate and frustrated argument. So long as the debate is verbal Pamela always wins; and despite Mr. B.'s attempts to gain her affection by kidnapping and imprisoning her she gradually achieves more and more real freedom. Whenever her exasperated master descends to more direct methods she is always saved by her 'happy knack at falling into fits'.

But the book is much more than a debate about the rights of women. Although Mr. B's wooing of his beautiful servant girl is conducted in terms of rights and duties, it is infused with powerful feeling. Whenever the two lovers come into each other's presence the emotional temperature rises immediately. There is little affection between them— their meetings almost always end in impotent fury on one side and tears on the other—but their attraction for each other, distorted and frustrated though it may be, is undoubtedly there. In this first novel there is considerable crudeness and naïvety in Richardson's presentation of sexual passion; and his characterization of Mr. B. can scarcely be called successful: as one contemporary critic remarked rather dryly, it is just as well that the author has informed us that Mr. B. 'had been a great rake, and had debauch'd several women . . . for from his whole behaviour towards his Pamela, one should be apt to think him the meerest novice in the world'. But despite the gaucheries both of Mr. B., and of Richardson himself, one cannot deny the strength and complexity of feeling which develops as the novel unfolds. Psychological realism such as this, though common enough in drama, was something new in English fiction, and it had an immediate appeal to the contemporary reading public. Even today the first section of *Pamela*, that in which the story of the courtship is told, can hold and excite the interest. Once the marriage has occurred, however, the tension disappears, and apart from one or two scenes the rest of the book, in which the preacher is allowed to take over almost completely from the novelist, is dull, worthless stuff.

Much of the power in the first part of *Pamela* arises from that suppressed and morbid sexual passion which burns like a slow fire beneath the surface of all this writer's work. But an equally important element in the complex of feelings which both inspired and were released by the writing of this and the other novels is Richardson's obsession with the moral and social problems of the rights of the individual. The two sets of feelings are, in fact, inextricably involved; the sexual conflict in his novels always reflects a social struggle of much wider significance. Pamela and Mr. B., like all Richardson's lovers, express their 'love' for each other in debates about rights and duties; and in one way the battle in which they are all involved is not sexual at all. Richardson's heroines are all democrats: their most fundamental desire is that their suitors should 'respect' them; that is, should accord them their rights as individual human beings before beginning to treat them as women. As Pamela says to Mr. B.,

> Whatever you have to propose, whatever you intend by me, let my assent be that of a free person, mean as I am, and not of a sordid slave, who is to be threatened and frightened into a compliance.

In a sense this is a denial of sex; and the way in which Pamela and Clarissa argue with their lovers and use tears and fits in an attempt to escape from the physical realities of the sexual situation is undoubtedly 'sentimental'. But from another point of view there is nothing sentimental at all in their attitude: Richardson's heroines have no illusions about the disadvantages of belonging to the weaker sex. As Anne Howe, who represents the voice of common sense in *Clarissa*, remarks, there is nothing very glorious in being 'cajoled, wire-drawn and ensnared, like silly birds into a state of bondage . . . courted as princesses for a few weeks, in order to be treated as slaves for the rest of our lives'. In a society dominated by men such ideas, especially when they are held by a mere maidservant as Pamela was, are socially rather embarrassing; and there can be no doubt that much of the ridicule which Richardson's first novel attracted, was aroused by the brilliant insubordination of his heroine. Parody is, more often than not, just as much an attempt to laugh an uncomfortable truth out of existence as it is to ridicule error, hypocrisy and dullness. *Shamela*'s most obvious target is the genuine sentimentality and hypocrisy of Richardson; but Fielding also wrote it in the effort to make Pamela *conform*, to force her into the more easily acceptable mould of the feminine fortune hunter. But Pamela is far too complicated to be forced into any pattern. Indeed it is because she refuses to fit into the usual pattern, refuses to behave like Moll Flanders or Roxana, that she becomes the first real heroine in English fiction.

Pamela's complexity reflects the complexity of Richardson himself. As Brian Downs has so aptly put it, he wrote from 'a divided heart'. And the divisions, the inner conflicts in Richardson's heart, are significant not simply because they provided the impetus for writing the novels, and generated the complex feeling with which they are charged, but also because they symbolized in a personal and dramatic form some of the most fundamental problems of the society in which he lived. Richardson's guilts and fears were the guilts and fears of his age; and when he turned his unwitting eyes in upon the dark corners of his own soul his readers felt that theirs were being exposed too. 'C'est lui,' wrote Diderot, 'qui porte le flambeau au fond de la caverne.'

Richardson was not a happy man. Craving affection he had learnt to mistrust it, and instead to pin all his hopes of emotional security on the exercise of power. 'There can be no love without fear!' he maintained: children must learn to respect their parents, and wives their husbands, before they can love them. Timid, lonely and socially diffident, he drew great satisfaction from the influence and respect which his position as a paterfamilias, a successful printer, and later a successful novelist brought him. Clearly he had a vested interest in trying to preserve those conventions of the social order in which his own small authority rested. Yet he was blessed (or cursed) with that primary innocence and honesty of vision which all great artists possess. If suffering or injustice existed he could not blind himself to them, nor, in the last resort, forgive himself for them, even when the suffering and injustice were the direct result of those aspects of the social structure which it was plainly in his own interest to leave undisturbed. Indeed these were the things which seemed to fascinate him most: although in real life he enjoyed exercising his rights as a man, a husband, a father and a bourgeois snob, in his novels he subjected the question of the validity of these rights to a most painful and searching examination.

His attitude to women, to children and to the family was essentially ambivalent: a compound of sympathy and hatred, arrogance and fear, pride and guilt. His sympathy for women, for instance, made him a passionate advocate of their rights; but at the same time his outraged and terrified male ego, in the nightmare figures of Mr. B., Lovelace, and the kind but implacable Grandison, ensured that the Pamelas and Clarissas of this world should be punished for their rebelliousness, and the Charlotte Grandisons and Harriet Byrons kept firmly in their place.

It seems clear that when Richardson began to write *Pamela* he had no great understanding or control of the conflicting inner forces he was about to release. In a very real sense he did not know what he was doing: almost without his realizing it his simple moral tract somehow turned into a novel. In the process he discovered his powers —but he did not discover how to organize and discipline them. Because of this the characterization and structure of his first novel are twisted out of shape, and the book as a whole displays most bewildering contradictions in tone and intention. But in the successful sections of the novel his ability, the promise of his genius, is clearly manifest. The source is obvious too: the most vital element in the book, the thing that made it so spectacularly successful in its own day, is its confused but angry concern with social injustice. And it is this rather than its psychological realism that makes it still readable: Pamela's arguments with Mr. B. are as lively and convincing today as when they were first written. But the most impressive scene in *Pamela* is one in which Mr. B. does not appear: it is the quarrel between Pamela and Mr. B.'s sister, Lady Davers. By an almost theatrical, but no doubt unconscious, contrivance Richardson is able in this scene to forget all those conventional notions of duty and decorum which lay a film of sentimentality and hypocrisy over so much of the novel. Lady Davers not only does not know that Pamela is her brother's wife, but she is completely unprepared to believe it. Pamela, however, knowing that she is indeed married, and therefore Lady Davers' social equal, is perfectly sure of her own position. Each of them is thus able to speak her mind with perfect honesty, without false condescension on the one hand or false humility on the other. The situation is electric: the dialogue, rapid and colloquial, crackles back and forth—Pamela's dignified but spirited defence of herself contrasting vividly with the passionate and spiteful raging of Lady Davers. It is an ugly and perhaps slightly hysterical scene, but it is savagely revealing. Its sheer dramatic power is undeniable: it is the most sustained piece of writing in *Pamela*, and one of the least cluttered or involved. Richardson's literary genius here breaks free completely from the restrictive patterns of puritan didactic literature; and it is patent that, given the right material and the right opportunities to develop it, he should be able to produce a work of fiction of considerable force and stature. In *Clarissa* this is what he does: and if the title means anything, it is *Clarissa*, rather than *Pamela* or *Joseph Andrews*, which should be called the first English novel.

III

'CLARISSA'

Clarissa, which was published in 1747–48, a year or more before *Tom Jones*, is the first English novel to have been conceived and planned from the beginning as a unified piece of what Henry James delighted to call 'fictive art'. Inspired and encouraged by the success of *Pamela*, and with his imagination fired by a theme which suited his genius perfectly, Richardson was determined to produce a work of literature that could be measured by the highest standards of art as well as of morality. And he succeeded: *Clarissa* is a great novel. One of its most impressive features—especially when it is compared with *Pamela*—is its structural coherence, its formal unity. The length of the novel has been criticized since it first appeared, perhaps with justice, but one must agree with the author himself when he claims that

> long as the Work is, there is not one Digression, not one Reflection, but what arises naturally from the Subject, and makes for it, and to carry it on.

There is nothing accidental or haphazard about *Clarissa*: it is a triumph of craft. But the care with which it has been constructed has not in any way stifled the inner vitality of the story. Although the multitude of incidents all dovetail together in a way that could only be the result of scrupulous planning, the action seems to develop organically towards its inevitable climax and conclusion: Lovelace's physical violation of Clarissa and her spiritual triumph and glorification.

Richardson's determination to carry his story through to its preordained end was quite unshakable: despite tearful pleas from his female admirers—and even requests from Cibber, Fielding and other men of letters—'to make what is called a Happy Ending', he never wavered from his tragic design. It is this inflexibility of purpose that makes *Clarissa* such a convincing and at times terrifying book: it moves forward as slowly and inexorably as a lava-flow, and with this movement the characters are caught up and borne irresistibly along. It is 'such a strange situation . . . we are in,' writes Clarissa apprehensively to her friend Anne Howe, on the eve of her abduction by Lovelace; '*strange* I may well call it . . . we seem all to be *impelled*, as it were, by a perverse fate, which none of us are able to resist.'

No-one, reading *Pamela*, could have predicted that its author would ever produce anything so comprehensive in scope and so formally satisfying as *Clarissa*. Richardson's attainment of artistic maturity was amazingly rapid. Moreover it was consciously and intelligently directed: he knew what he was doing when he wrote his second novel. Like Fielding, whose discussions of the principles of his art are one of the pleasantest features of *Tom Jones*, Richardson evolved a theory of fiction to justify and explain his practice. Unfortunately he lacked Fielding's knowledge of the traditions of literature and literary criticism; he had to turn to friends like Joseph Spence, and the poets Edward Young and Aaron Hill, for assistance in working out his ideas, and his projected critical Preface for *Clarissa* never got beyond the stage of a rough draft, although he did include some of his ideas, in a less trenchant form, in the *Postscript* he added to the final version of the novel. It is a pity that he was not able to give a conclusive shape to his theory of the novel, for it is sophisticated and perceptive, and much closer to what we now believe to be the truth about the essential nature of this literary form than Fielding's theory of the comic epic poem in prose. He shared with Fielding the belief that the novel should be realistic, and should concern itself with the lives of ordinary people: as one of his friends put it, 'the workings of private and domestic Passions', are his subject, not the 'imaginary Adventures of Kings, Heroes, Heroines'. But Richardson was also convinced—convinced as thoroughly as Henry James was to be one hundred and fifty years later —that the novel was at its best when it was most dramatic. His main concern in all his novels is not so much to tell a story as to present and explore particular situations, situations which could conceivably occur 'in a private Family', and which raised the moral issues and problems which were significant both for himself and for society as a whole. The closest realism and the most thorough examination of the situation was his aim; and he felt that this could be obtained best 'not in the narrative way', that is, not by writing about the people involved, but by letting them speak for themselves,

> by making them write their own thoughts to Friends, soon after each Incident happened; with all that Naturalness and Warmth, with which they felt them, at that Time, in their own Minds.

Thus he justifies his use of the epistolary way of writing fiction; and he asserts that there is no need to insist on 'the evident Superiority of this Method to the dry Narrative'.

The advantages of the epistolary method are indisputable; in *Clarissa* the reader is kept more continuously and intensely aware both of the action and the people involved in it than in *Tom Jones* —'the characters', in Richardson's words, 'sink deeper into the Mind of the Reader'. Moreover this technique enables the writer to present the moral and emotional problems with which his characters are faced in very fine detail: the slightest nuances of feeling, the subtlest shades of discrimination, can be captured, the web and texture of experience, of moment to moment living, can be suggested if not fully rendered. But although the epistolary method permits the writer to achieve all this one cannot deny its inherent clumsiness and implausibility. Recent and contemporary novelists like James, Proust, Joyce and Faulkner, to mention but a few, have learnt how to attain similar effects in more realistic and less obviously artificial ways; and the technical apparatus used by Richardson seems primitive and awkward by comparison.

Nevertheless his use of the letter form can, especially in *Clarissa*, be accepted as a convention no more essentially unrealistic than blank verse, the stream of consciousness technique, or the use of song in opera. And it can be accepted because it is something more than a mere literary device. For Richardson it is a technique which reflects perfectly the themes with which he is preoccupied. Indeed it is doubtful whether any other contemporary fictional form would have enabled him to allow such full expression to his genius, for the epistolary novel gives the author a unique opportunity for presenting and examining the inner lives of his characters—and Richardson is pre-eminently concerned with the moral significance of the inner life.

His main characters are all placed in situations in which they are forced to defend their personal integrity. Richardson was a conventional man; but he also believed profoundly in the right of the individual to make up his own mind in matters of morality, to be like Sir Charles Grandison, his ideal hero, and live 'to himself, and to his own heart, rather than to the opinion of the world'. But the forces of convention often come into conflict with the free moral conscience; and it was just this aspect of life that Richardson, himself deeply committed to both sides of the struggle, found most fascinating. Pamela and Clarissa, and to a smaller degree many of his other characters, have to fight for the privilege of being able to follow the dictates of their own consciences —Clarissa, in fact, sacrifices her life in the process.

At one level the battle is fought out overtly between the individual and the members of the various social groups to whom he or she owes allegiance: Clarissa, for instance, has one struggle with her family, another with Lovelace, and the world he represents, and a third with society as a whole. But the most bitter conflicts are those which go on at a deeper level in the hearts of the characters themselves: Clarissa is torn cruelly between her love for and loyalty to her parents, her tormented and frustrated passion for Lovelace, and her profound conviction that she has every right to resist their efforts to make her own decisions for her. It is this 'war of duties' within the individual personality, together with 'the delineation of . . . subtlety of feeling . . .

[and] entanglements of delicacy', which Henry Mackenzie, in 1785, pronounced to be the distinguishing feature of the sentimental novel.

Since the latter half of the eighteenth century Richardson has been described as a sentimental novelist; and to those readers who are acquainted only with *Pamela* the title may seem more than justified. But when Mackenzie described 'that species [of novel] called the sentimental', the word 'sentimental' carried little of that connotation of shallowness, excess and insincerity which it bears today. When Richardson's reputation stood highest a sentimental novel was understood to be one in which the moral sentiments of the characters were presented and analysed with some care and seriousness. Sentimental in this sense *Clarissa* certainly is; and except for the over-long conclusion, and perhaps for the fact that Clarissa has to die at all, it is marred by little of that false sentimentality which so disfigures *Pamela*. *Clarissa* is a mercilessly realistic and profoundly sad exposure of human behaviour.

Indeed one of its fundamental themes is the tragic ineffectiveness of any view of life which is sentimental in the sense of being foolishly optimistic. In the Preface to the third edition of *Clarissa* Richardson states that the first of his intentions in writing the novel is

> to warn the inconsiderate and thoughtless of the one sex against the base arts and designs of specious contrivers of the other.

And *Clarissa* is above everything else a warning: a warning to the credulous, the idealistic, and the trustful—a warning not only against putting one's trust in rakes, but against putting one's trust in anyone or anything except, ultimately, one's own conscience and judgement. Clarissa is not destroyed by the libertine Lovelace, she is destroyed by the forces of convention—forces which work almost as strongly within her own heart as they do in the society in which she moves. Her family, who are ordinary, conventional people, distorted into monsters of cruelty by their weakness and their lust

for power and money, humiliate her and force her to elope
with Lovelace because she refuses to submit to the hypocrisy
of a marriage without love. But she also brings destruction
on herself because, in her own heart, she cannot finally
deny the authority of her family, and because she refuses to
face up to the realities of her relationship with Lovelace. It
is Clarissa's determination not to recognize the suspicious
aspects of the situation in which Lovelace involves her in
London which compensates for and in part explains the
apparent implausibility of this part of the novel. As one of
the earliest critics of *Clarissa* remarked, it is doubtful

> whether probability has been preserved in the detestable audacity of
> Lovelace; to carry a lady of quality to a brothel, to confine her captive
> there against her will, to give her opium, and to violate her person.

In one sense the situation is obviously incredible; but, at the
psychological level it is not: Clarissa is more securely
enmeshed in the web of her own conventional illusions than
in all Lovelace's plots. As Dr. Johnson remarked, there is
always something she prefers to truth. At one level the
novel is an account of seduction and rape—at another it
is the story of the pitiless awakening of a conventional
young woman, a 'nice girl', to the realities of life. Circumstances conspire cruelly against Clarissa to shatter one
by one the illusions she cherishes—that parents 'naturally'
love their children, that no man with any human feeling
can be utterly cruel, that love is always stronger than lust
or greed. The final blow is struck when, after a long
process of deception and subtle torture, Lovelace violates
her.

There is a sense in which Clarissa, like all sentimental
heroines, asks to be raped. Her prudery (which Lovelace, in
his perverted fashion, both flaunts and encourages) forces
her to deny the sexual facts of the situation in which she is
involved; and the treatment she receives at his hands is in part
a savage masculine retaliation for her prim coldness ('Dear
creature!' Lovelace exclaims in despairing admiration. 'Did

she never romp?') At another level it can be regarded as a
punishment inflicted by society on an individual who has
dared to be unconventional. Clarissa herself looks at it in this
way, seeing in it the fulfilment of her father's curse, a reward
for her filial impiety. But the significance of the rape and of
the rôle Lovelace plays in it, is more complex than this.
Lovelace is one of the most remarkable characters in English
fiction. In some ways he is an implausible monster, an
unhappy blend of literature and life—a 'fancy piece' as Mrs.
Barbauld calls him. But he is a fancy piece endowed by
Richardson's imagination with a fierce inextinguishable
vitality; and it is clear that, like Milton's Satan, he partly
escaped from his creator's control and assumed a life of his
own. He is not all villain: one of his most important functions
in the novel is to act as the voice of reason and scepticism,
and he is not an altogether unworthy representative of the
intellectual side of aristocratic libertinism. He hates the
Harlowes for their canting hypocrisy; and he despises them
for their parvenu values and their crudely obvious attempts
at social climbing. And Clarissa, by her refusal to admit that
he is justified in his opinion of her family, puts herself in the
position of defending the very attitudes and beliefs against
which she has been struggling herself, and which have, in
effect, driven her into his arms. The rape is thus not merely a
personal attack on Clarissa, but an attack on the conventional values which her family and, in part, herself
represent: it is the most violent expression of that hatred of
middle-class hypocrisy and materialism by which so much
of the novel is animated. It is also the physical culmination
and symbol of that brutal process of awakening through
which Clarissa has been made to go: Lovelace, the Hobbesian
man of reason, forces her to acknowledge the truth about
herself and other people.

But, paradoxically enough, in doing so he destroys
himself. The rape, committed while Clarissa is drugged, is
a token rape only, a confession of impotence not a demon-
stration of power, an expression of rage at his failure to

arouse in her the love he really craves. Clarissa, however, is spiritually liberated by the event, even though it results, rather implausibly, in her subsequent death. After this ultimate act of betrayal she has no illusions left: the persons from whom she has had every right to expect kindness and loyalty—her family and her lover—have deserted and abused her; the ideals in which she has put her faith have all, save one, been destroyed. Her faith in her own personal integrity is still unshaken: if anything it is now stronger than ever. Few people have been compelled so cruelly to face the unpleasant facts of human nature as Clarissa; but when the last shreds of illusion have been torn away she accepts the situation with honesty and courage. It is one of the great moments in English literature when, defying not only her seducer but also her family and the whole world of conventional respectability, she cries out to Lovelace: 'The man who has been the villain to me you have been, shall never make me his wife!'

Lovelace is a terrifying enough figure, but he is a cardboard horror compared with the Harlowes. The opening scenes of the novel in which the slowly deepening conflict between Clarissa and her family is presented have an extraordinary power. As Clarissa's determination not to let herself be sacrificed to the ruthless ambition of her brother hardens, the motives of the rest of the family begin to stand out in their true colours. Shame at the knowledge that they are in the wrong only makes them act with gradually increasing cruelty and anger towards the girl they pretend to love. The characterization is masterly: the brother and sister, utterly vulgar and selfish, and the basically kind but pathetically weak mother, are clearly imagined and most convincingly portrayed. The father is a figure of tremendous psychological force: incapacitated and embittered by illness he has let the management of the family fall into the hands of his arrogant son, and Clarissa rarely sees him. But he is still a terrifying symbol of parental authority: she receives his commands like distant thunderings from Mount Sinai,

and the curse he hurls after her as she flees with Lovelace
haunts her to her deathbed.

As the action develops the atmosphere slowly becomes
more and more claustrophobic: every door Clarissa turns
to is locked, every member of her family whom she asks for
help and sympathy rejects her. Even her attempts to state her
case reasonably to her parents are continually frustrated:
she knows before she begins that her arguments will be
useless whatever happens. 'I will hear what you have to say,'
says her mother, in one of their tortured interviews, 'but
with this intimation, that say what you will, it will be of no
avail elsewhere.' Her words are continually twisted against
her, and everything she does and says is interpreted as
evidence, not of her dislike of the repulsive Solmes, but of
her love for Lovelace. As the frustrating and agonizingly
repetitive arguments go on Clarissa becomes bewildered,
angry and finally terrified. She slowly realizes that, incredible
as it may seem, there is not one person amongst her sup-
posedly loving family who has either enough sympathy or
enough courage to come to her defence. And even though
she becomes more and more strongly convinced that her
passive defiance of her parents is morally justified, she cannot
allow herself to forget that she is technically guilty of filial
impiety. This impasse in which she finds herself generates an
atmosphere of bafflement, fear and maddening frustration
which becomes more and more nightmarish. And in the
true nightmare fashion, when she does try to escape, the
sanctuary in which she seeks refuge turns out to be even
more horrible than the terrors from which she flees: she
places herself in the hands of a man who is much more
ruthlessly determined to ruin her than her family ever were.

In the opening sections of *Clarissa* there is an intensity
which one finds hardly anywhere else in the English novel.
Though he is a lesser writer than either of them, it is perhaps
of Dostoievski and Kafka that Richardson here reminds us
most strongly. In no other English writer of comparable
stature do we find the same obsessive preoccupation with

the problems of guilt and cruelty, or such a bleak and terrifying vision of the lonely battle which must be fought out
by the person who wishes to preserve the right to make his
own moral decisions. 'What a world is this!' cries Clarissa in
despair and perplexity.

> What is there in it desirable? The good one hopes for so strangely
> mixed, that one knows not what to wish for! And one half of man-
> kind tormenting the other, and being tormented themselves in
> tormenting!

The picture of suffering humanity which is presented in
Clarissa is profoundly sad. It is also in some ways narrow
and limited: there are qualities in life to which Richardson
was completely insensitive. But the picture is unforgettable:
Clarissa leaves its mark indelibly on the mind of the reader
as only the greatest novels can.

IV

'SIR CHARLES GRANDISON'

Having presented the world with the portrait of a good woman in *Clarissa*, Richardson was urged by his friends to produce a novel about a good man. He did not need a great deal of encouragement: in 1753–54 he published *The History of Sir Charles Grandison*. It was respectfully received by the public and the critics, but in many ways it is the least successful of his three novels. The hero, Sir Charles Grandison himself, has become a byword for priggish and pompous virtue; and the book itself, huge, slack and nerveless, lacks both the unity and the tension of *Clarissa*, and possesses little of the vigour and liveliness of the much cruder *Pamela*. Yet it contains some of Richardson's best writing and in certain respects it played a more important part in the development of the novel than anything else he wrote.

The first portion of the novel is the best and it was also the most influential. It deals with a situation which was to become one of those most favoured by the novelists, especially the women novelists, who followed Richardson; a situation, moreover, which in the hands of Jane Austen and later Henry James, was to prove highly rewarding. Fanny Burney, the first important successor to Richardson, described the situation best, perhaps, when she gave the sub-title of *A Young Lady's Entrance into the World* to her first novel, *Evelina*. It is a subject especially rich in satiric possibilities, and in the first part of *Sir Charles Grandison*, which deals with the introduction of Harriet Byron into London society, Richardson takes full advantage of them. This portion of the novel is written with a lightness of touch and a feeling for wit and comedy that are as admirable as they are unexpected. His presentation of Harriet's encounters with her various suitors, especially the villain of the piece, Sir Hargrave Pollexfen, is remarkably polished. Richardson's portraits of men from the women's standpoint are often astonishingly penetrating. From the outside at least his rakes are always convincing: arrogant, selfish, ignorant of love, amazed and incredulous at the spectacle of a woman's having a mind of her own, and altogether unable to comprehend that someone could dislike them. Sir Hargrave is no exception: this is how Harriet describes one of his attempts at courtship:

Had not Sir Hargrave intended me an honour, and had he not a very high opinion of the efficacy of eight thousand pounds a year in an address of this kind, I dare say, he would have supposed a little more prefacing necessary: But, after he had told me, in a few words, how much he was attracted by my character before he saw me, he thought fit to refer himself directly to the declaration he had made at Lady Betty Williams's . . . then talked of large settlements; boasted of his violent passion; and besought my favour with the utmost earnestness. . . . I thought it best to answer him with openness and unreserve.

To seem to question the sincerity of such professions as you make, Sir Hargrave, might appear to you as if I want to be assured: But, be pleased to know you are directing your discourse to one of the plainest-hearted women in England. . . . I thank you, Sir, for your good opinion of me; but I cannot encourage your addresses.

You *cannot*, madam, *encourage my addresses*! And express yourself so seriously! Good Heaven! . . . I have been assured, madam, recovering a little from his surprise, that your affections are not engaged. But, surely, it must be a mistake: Some happy man—

Is it, interrupted I, a necessary consequence, that the woman who cannot receive the addresses of Sir Hargrave Pollexfen, must be engaged?

Why, madam—as to that—I know not what to say—But a man of my fortune, and, I hope, not *absolutely* disagreeable either in person or temper; of *some* rank in life—He paused; then resuming—What, madam, if you are as much in earnest as you seem, can be your objection? . . .

We do not, we *cannot*, all like the same person. . . .

Social comedy of this sort had not appeared in the English novel before; but once the vein had been opened it was to be exploited with increasing frequency and success. *Sir Charles Grandison* is the direct ancestor of the novels of Jane Austen; and it is not surprising to learn that Richardson

was one of her favourite authors. According to her nephew
J. E. Austen-Leigh,

> Her knowledge of Richardson's works was such as no-one is likely
> again to acquire, now that the multitudes and merits of our light
> literature have called off the attention of readers from that great
> master. Every circumstance narrated in Sir Charles Grandison, all
> that was ever said or done in the cedar parlour, was familiar to her;
> and the wedding days of Lady L. and Lady G. were as well remem-
> bered as if they had been living friends.

How are we to account for the unusual excellence of the
opening sections of *Grandison*? There are, I think, two main
reasons. One is that, in this part of the novel, Richardson has
no particular moral axe to grind. The impossibly stiff and
virtuous Sir Charles has not yet appeared, and the author's
only concern is to paint a convincing picture of the life of a
quiet but fashionable young woman: the atmosphere is
light and—strange word to use in connection with
Richardson!—happy. But a more important reason is that
Harriet Byron is a completely independent person: the
type towards which all Richardson's heroines have been
tending. As she tells Sir Hargrave:

> If I do not meet with a man to whom I can give my whole heart, I
> never will marry at all. . . . You are angry, Sir Hargrave. . . but you
> have no right to be so. You address me as one who is her own mistress.

If Pamela or Clarissa had been able to say this there would
have been no novels written about them—but how much
happier they would have been! Harriet, a wealthy orphan,
is free from the social obligations against which they have
to struggle. She can be honest with herself where they cannot,
and being conveniently detached from society she is able to
criticize it with impunity. She is the only really likeable
character Richardson ever created: she lacks the sentimentality of Pamela and the stiffness of Clarissa, and
though she may be waspish she is free alike from the hardness
of Anne Howe and the vulgarity of Charlotte Grandison. It
is obvious that she is the model on whom Fanny Burney's

Evelina is based; and there are traces of her lineaments to be found in Elizabeth Bennett and Marianne Dashwood, not to mention the heroines of countless minor novels now deservedly forgotten.

The promise held out in the first two hundred pages of *Sir Charles Grandison* is unfortunately not fulfilled. With the introduction of the hero Richardson's moral earnestness re-asserts itself. The appearance of Sir Charles on the scene, however, is very skilfully stage-managed: in his first brush with Sir Hargrave he cuts a dashing and gallant figure. But although he saves Harriet from being ruined by Sir Hargrave he quite effectively ruins her in another way himself. As soon as she begins to play heroine to Sir Charles's hero, poor Harriet loses her sparkle and becomes a dull girl indeed. The rest of the novel, though admirable in many ways, is on the whole insipid. Virtue triumphant is never as interesting as virtue in distress, and when, as in *Sir Charles Grandison*, it consistently triumphs through several volumes it becomes positively boring.

Not only is *Sir Charles Grandison* boring, but also it is often deliberately sentimental and sensational as *Pamela* and *Clarissa* rarely are. In *Clarissa*, even though the emotional force of the novel arises naturally out of the basic theme and situation, Richardson had discovered that he possessed to a remarkable degree the power of playing on the feelings of his readers. And in his last novel he often obviously contrives effects that seem to have been previously achieved with unselfconscious spontaneity. Pathetic figures like Emily Jervois and Clementina della Poretta are used to bring tears to the reader's eyes; and Sir Hargrave Pollexfen, a pale shadow of Lovelace, exists mainly for the purpose of producing easy thrills. These characters and the sentimental and violent situations in which they appeared were to be imitated over and over again in the cheap and degenerate novels of sentiment that were produced in such numbers during the next thirty or forty years. But if Richardson is partly responsible for inspiring some of the most worthless fiction ever written in England he also inspired some of the best; and the influence of *Sir Charles Grandison* on the technique of the novel is incalculable. It is surely one of the most naturalistic of all novels; and the exposition and resolution of its vast and complicated plot are conducted with unobtrusive skill. The only trouble is that the characters themselves are very ordinary and uninteresting people; and the situations in which they are involved are not in general of sufficient significance to engage the full attention of the reader—especially the modern reader. Like its hero the novel is undoubtedly worthy: it is also unquestionably dull.

RICHARDSON'S RANGE

Dull but worthy: the verdict can certainly be applied with justice to *Sir Charles Grandison* and to long stretches of Richardson's other novels. But it can by no means be applied to his work as a whole. An artist deserves to be judged by his best achievement: and *Clarissa* is a masterpiece. It towers above most of the other novels of the century, and it exhibits, as neither *Pamela* nor *Sir Charles Grandison* does, Richardson's particular abilities consistently employed to their fullest advantage; for although he is a great novelist he is very much the novelist of one book.

What are Richardson's peculiar talents? What are the qualities which give his work greatness, and which distinguish it from the work of other novelists? One of them certainly is his sentimentalism, his ability to analyse and present with subtlety, exactness and sympathy the changing thoughts and feelings of his characters. Like Proust and James he has the power of making the reader intensely and continuously aware of the myriad significances of apparently simple human situations; and of suggesting, with innumerable delicate strokes, the variety and complexity of the human personality, and the mystery that lies at its core. We are compelled to read *Clarissa* by curiosity as much as anything else. Richardson manages somehow simultaneously to excite and frustrate the reader's attention: for as long as is possible the situation is kept unresolved, the tension and suspense are maintained and intensified. In this atmosphere of quivering sensibilities the lightest touch may be loaded with incalculable meanings; and a whisper may break in with the violence of a thunderclap. Morbid, stifling, dreamlike—*Clarissa* has all these qualities: but it is undeniably fascinating.

It is also undeniably realistic. At the most superficial level there is the Hogarthian vigour of scenes like the death of Mrs. Sinclair (which the Abbé Prevost paid Richardson the compliment of omitting, together with several other passages, from his translation of the novel because he considered them too strong for French taste). Equally impressive, though sometimes tedious, is the exhaustive thoroughness with which he has traced out every thread in the complex relationship—financial and legal as well as emotional—by which the characters are bound to each other and on which so much of the plot depends. We know more about the people in Richardson's novels than we do about most people in real life; and there are few other novelists who attempt to present such a complete picture of a human situation.

Richardson's realism and his sentimentalism are at bottom the same: his preoccupation with the details, both psychological and material, of his characters' lives, is the strongest expression of that desire for the truth, the urge to come to terms with himself and with human problems that were his concern, by which he was obsessed. The range of his vision is narrow, it is true, but in *Clarissa* he achieves an analytical rendering of a human situation which is at once extraordinarily comprehensive and profoundly moving. *Clarissa* perhaps lacks nobility—her virtue, after all, is of the passive kind; and after reading the novel we are left with a heightened awareness not of man's potentiality for good and great actions but of his capacity for meanness and his ability to inflict pain on others and on himself. We admire the courage of *Clarissa*, but our admiration is not so strong as our feeling of despair and outrage, our feeling that no-one should be allowed to suffer as she has suffered, our realization that humanity needs protecting more strongly from itself than from anything else. *Clarissa* certainly has its limitations; but the vision of life it offers is a valid and necessary one. With all its faults it remains a great novel, and the only major work of fiction of tragic dimensions produced during the eighteenth century.

SAMUEL RICHARDSON

Select Bibliography

BIBLIOGRAPHIES

SALE, W. M. *Samuel Richardson: A Bibliographical Record of His Literary Career with Historical Notes*. New Haven: Yale University Press, 1936. The standard bibliography.

CORDASCO, F. *Samuel Richardson: A List of Critical Studies Published from 1896 to 1946*. Brooklyn: Long Island University Press, 1948.

SALE, W. M. *Samuel Richardson: Master Printer*. Ithaca, N. Y.: Cornell University Press, 1950.
There is a long bibliography in A. D. McKillop, *Samuel Richardson*—see below.

COLLECTED EDITIONS

The Works. With a Sketch of his Life and Writings by the Rev. E. Mangin. 19 vols. London: Miller, 1811.

The Novels. With a Memoir of the Life of the Author by Sir Walter Scott. Ballantyne's Novelist's Library. 3 vols. London: Hurst, 1824.

The Works. With a Prefatory Chapter of Biographical Criticism by Leslie Stephen. 12 vols. London: Sotheran, 1883–1884.

The Novels. With a Life of the Author and Introductions by W. L. Phelps. 19 vols. New York: Croscup and Sterling, 1901–1902.

The Novels. With an Introduction by E. M. M. McKenna. 20 vols. London: Chapman, 1902.

The Novels. Shakespeare Head Edition. 18 vols. Oxford: Blackwell, 1929–1931.

LETTERS

The Correspondence of Samuel Richardson. Edited by Anna L. Barbauld. 6 vols. London: Phillips, 1804.
The only collection of Richardson's letters published in book form.

The bulk, which are still unprinted, are in the Forster Collection in the Victoria and Albert Museum, London.

SEPARATE WORKS

Note. Dates of original London editions are given. Modern editions and paperbacks are also recorded here.

Letters Written to and for Particular Friends, on the Most Important Occasions, 1741.

Reprinted, with an introduction by B. W. Downs, as *Familiar Letters on Important Occasions* (New York: Dodd, Mead, 1928).

Pamela: Or Virtue Rewarded. Part I, 1740; Part II, 1741.

The text used in all modern reprints is that of the sixth edition, 1742, which Richardson had revised considerably. Everyman's Library, 2 vols.; Norton Paperback.

Clarissa: Or, The History of a Young Lady, 1748.

The standard text is that of the fourth edition, 1751. Preface by Anna Barbauld (The British Novelists, 1810); Everyman's Library, 4 vols.; Modern Library.

Meditations Collected from the Sacred Books—Being Those Mentioned in the History of Clarissa, 1750.

Letters and Passages Restored from the Original Manuscript of the History of Clarissa, 1751.

The History of Sir Charles Grandison, 1754.

The standard text is that of the third edition, 1754.

A Collection of the Moral and Instructive Sentiments . . . Contained in : . . Pamela, Clarissa, *and* Sir Charles Grandison, 1755.

BIOGRAPHICAL AND CRITICAL STUDIES

FIELDING, SARAH (?). *Remarks on Clarissa.* London: Robinson, 1749.

Critical Remarks on Sir Charles Grandison, Clarissa, *and* Pamela. By a Lover of Virtue. London: Dowse, 1754.

Reprinted in facsimile by The Augustan Reprint Society, 1950.

DIDEROT, D. "Eloge de Richardson," *Le Journal Etranger* (January, 1762). A famous tribute to Richardson's genius, containing some extravagant but illuminating criticism.

DOBSON, AUSTIN. *Samuel Richardson.* English Men of Letters. New York: Macmillan, 1902.

DOWNS, BRIAN W. *Richardson.* New York: Dutton, 1928.

KRUTCH, JOSEPH WOOD. *Five Masters: Boccaccio, Cervantes, Richardson, Stendhal, Proust.* New York: Cape and Smith, 1931.

DOTTIN, PAUL. *Samuel Richardson 1689–1761, Imprimeur de Londres, Auteur de* Pamela, Clarisse *et* Grandison. Paris: Perrin, 1931.

BOAS, F. S. *From Richardson to Pinero.* London: Murray, 1936.
Contains a chapter on Richardson's novels and their influence.

MCKILLOP, A. D. *Samuel Richardson, Printer and Novelist.* Chapel Hill, N. C.: University of North Carolina Press, 1936.
The standard work on Richardson.

PRITCHETT, V. S. *The Living Novel.* London: Chatto and Windus, 1946.
Contains a consideration of *Clarissa.*

HILL, C. "Clarissa Harlowe and Her Times," *Essays in Criticism,* Vol. V (October, 1955).

DAICHES, DAVID. *Literary Essays.* New York: Philosophical Library, 1957.
Contains an essay on *Clarissa.*

GOLDEN, M. *Richardson's Characters.* Coral Gables: University of Miami Press, 1963.

PARODIES AND ANTI-PAMELAS

FIELDING, HENRY (?). *An Apology for the Life of Mrs. Shamela Andrews.* London: Dodd, 1741.
Edited by Ian Watt (Augustan Reprint Society, 1956)—see also below, p. 73.

HAYWOOD, E. (?). *Anti-Pamela: Or, Feign'd Innocence Detected.* London: Huggonson, 1741.

POVEY, CHARLES. *The Virgin in Eden: Or, The State of Innocency.* London: Roberts, 1741.

FIELDING, HENRY. *The History of the Adventures of Joseph Andrews, and of his Friend Mr. Abraham Adams.* London: Millar, 1742.
May be considered as in part a parody of *Pamela.*

KREISSMAN, BERNARD. *Pamela-Shamela: A Study of the Criticisms, Burlesques, Parodies, and Adaptions of Richardson's "Pamela."* Lincoln: University of Nebraska Press, 1960.

HENRY FIELDING

by John Butt

HENRY FIELDING

From a sketch by *Hogarth* used as a frontispiece to the *Works*, 1762

HENRY FIELDING was born at Sharpham Park near Glastonbury on April 22, 1707. He died at Lisbon on October 8, 1754, and is there buried, in the English Cemetery.

FIELDING

I

To say that the English novel began in the seventeen-forties with the work of Richardson and Fielding is to invite refinement, if not contradiction. The Elizabethans had plenty of novels to read, by Nashe, Greene, Lodge, and Deloney; in the latter half of the seventeenth century there were numerous translations and imitations of the French romance; and Mrs. Behn, Defoe, and Mrs. Manley have all some claims upon the historian of the novel. Yet there is something in the broad contention which Richardson and Fielding, for all their differences, would have approved. Recalling the circumstances of his writing *Pamela* (1740) Richardson claimed, in a letter to a friend, that he had hit upon 'a new species of writing', and Fielding was equally confident that *Joseph Andrews* (1742) was a 'kind of writing, which I do not remember to have seen hitherto attempted in our language'. At least some of their readers were prepared to acknowledge the claim. Dr. Johnson, writing in 1750, when *Clarissa*, *Tom Jones*, and Smollett's *Roderick Random* had also been published, was able to distinguish one important difference between the new style of fiction and the old. In *Rambler* No. 4, he remarks that:

> The works of fiction, with which the present generation seems more particularly delighted, are such as exhibit life in its true state, diversified only by accidents that daily happen in the world, and influenced by passions and qualities which are really to be found in conversing with mankind. . . . Its province is to bring about natural events by easy means, and to keep up curiosity without the help of wonder: it is therefore precluded from the machines and expedients of the heroick romance, and can neither employ giants to snatch away a lady from the nuptial rites, nor knights to bring her back from captivity; it can neither bewilder its personages in deserts, nor lodge them in imaginary castles.

Such, Johnson would have us believe, were the themes and incidents of the older style of fiction. All the writer had to do was to 'let loose his invention, and heat his mind with incredibilities; a book was thus produced without fear of criticism, without the toil of study, without knowledge of nature, or acquaintance with life'. Very different, in Johnson's opinion, was the equipment of the modern novelist. Besides 'learning which is to be gained from books', he must have 'experience which ... must arise from general converse and accurate observation of the living world'; his books will then be not merely 'just copies of human manners', but they will also serve as 'lectures of conduct, and introductions into life'.

Perhaps Johnson was not altogether fair to the older style of fiction. Many novelists from the time of Sidney onwards had been interested in providing 'lectures of conduct'; and many besides Defoe (whom Johnson seems to have overlooked) were acquainted with life. But one of the principal differences between the old and the new he has made very clear in his emphasis upon 'accidents that daily happen in the world': the men and women in the novels of Fielding—and Richardson—act 'in such scenes of the universal drama as may be the lot of any other man' or woman. That is true of neither Sidney nor Defoe. A young man might imagine himself feeling like Sidney's Musidorus or acting like Robinson Crusoe; but he could never expect to share their experiences, as he might expect to share the experiences of Tom Jones. A young woman might well believe all that Moll Flanders reports had happened to her; but she could scarcely say of Moll, as she could say of Amelia or even of Clarissa, 'there but for the grace of God go I'.

But when Fielding, Richardson, and Johnson insisted that such accidents as 'daily happen in the world' must be the staple of the new style of fiction, they were writing not at the beginning but towards the end of a critical tradition. The marvellous had long been losing in esteem, and writers of romances in the previous century had been accustomed to discuss in their prefaces to what use historical incidents might be put. Thus Sir George Mackenzie, in the preface to his *Aretina* (1660), had censured those who have 'stuffed their Books with things impracticable, which because they were above the reach of man's power, they should never have fallen within the circle of his observation'; and Robert Boyle took credit for having chosen an episode from history for his *Theodora* (1687), since:

> True Examples do arm and fortify the mind far more efficaciously than Imaginary or Fictitious ones can do; and the fabulous labours of *Hercules*, and Exploits of *Arthur* of *Britain*, will never make men aspire to Heroick Vertue half so powerfully, as the real Examples of Courage and Gallantry afforded by *Jonathan*, *Cæsar*, or the *Black Prince*.

These novelists were following in the steps of de Scudéry, the most famous of the French romance writers, whose *Ibrahim* (1641) had been translated into English in 1652. In the preface to that work de Scudéry claimed that he had observed:

> the Manners, Customs, Religions, and Inclinations of People: and to give a more true resemblance to things, I have made the foundations of my work Historical, my principal Personages such as are marked out in the true History for illustrious persons.

Even though the practice of these writers did not always accord with their theory, it is easy to see how in time the desire for 'a more true resemblance to things' could lead the author of *Robinson Crusoe* to declare that 'the Editor believes the thing to be a just History of Fact; neither is there any Appearance of Fiction in it'. The innocent deception of passing off fiction as history or biography is perpetrated in several title-pages. Thus the reader is offered *The Life and Strange Surprising Adventures of Robinson Crusoe, of York, Mariner. Written by Himself*, or *The Fortunes and Misfortunes of the Famous Moll Flanders. Who was Born in Newgate, was Twelve Year a Thief, Eight Year a Transported Felon in Virginia. Written from her Memorandums.* Twenty years later the novelists were less concerned for the success of their deceptions. *Pamela, or Virtue Rewarded* is merely *A narrative which has its foundations in Truth and Nature;* but the tradition of offering 'a more true resemblance to things' is maintained in such titles as *The History of the Adventures of Joseph Andrews and of his friend Mr. Abraham Adams; Clarissa. Or, The History of a Young Lady; The History of Tom Jones, a Foundling.*

In choosing to let their novels pass as histories or biographies, these writers were aware of what they might adopt in structure and narrative technique from a well-established literary 'kind', and it is not surprising that they should search for profitable analogies in other forms of narrative as well. It was certainly to be expected that they would have an eye to the epic in particular, since this was a form of paramount reputation and one to the analysis of whose constituent parts much critical thought had been given. Sidney had long ago declared that the *Theagenes and Cariclea* of Heliodorus was not prevented from exerting influence as an heroic poem though it was written in prose, and he had set an example when revising his *Arcadia* to make its structure conform more truly to epic principles. De Scudéry again had emphasized what valuable lessons a novelist might learn from the epic, and possibly the most successful of modern epics, Fénelon's *Les Aventures de Télémaque*, had been written in prose. Thus when Fielding told his readers that *Joseph Andrews* was to be regarded as 'a comic epic poem in prose' and that this, moreover, was a 'kind of writing which I do not remember to have seen hitherto attempted in our language', the novelty of his claim lay not so much in the notion of a prose epic, nor even of a comic epic poem—for this everyone recognized in Pope's *Dunciad*—but in a conflation of the two. And though the act of conflation required the spark of Fielding's genius, the critical temper of the day was prepared to see such a spark fly.

II

Fielding himself was also well prepared for this new venture by his experience of men and books, and by his previous career as a writer. He came of a family of small landowners in the West Country related to the Earls of Denbigh: amongst his immediate forebears we find men who had risen to positions of some distinction in the learned professions. It might be suspected that the novelist derived his inclination towards the law from his mother's father, who was a Justice of the Queen's Bench, and that to his paternal grandfather, an archdeacon of Salisbury, he owed both his love of learning and the strong bent towards Christian moral teaching which characterize his novels. Though we need not pay too much attention to such surmises nor enquire what traits of character were inherited from his somewhat feckless father, Lieutenant-General Edmund Fielding, it is at least clear in what rank of society he was bred.

After a boyhood spent on his mother's Dorsetshire estates he joined his father in London, and in 1728, at the early age of twenty-one, he wrote his first play, *Love in Several Masques*, a comedy of manners. Partly no doubt owing to the patronage of his cousin, Lady Mary Wortley Montagu, the play was performed at Drury Lane Theatre, and ran for four nights. But though he was to lead a busy life as a dramatist and theatre-manager between 1730 and 1737, Fielding now decided not to pursue his moderate success but to enrol as a student in the Faculty of Letters at the University of Leyden under the redoubtable critic Peter Burmann. In later years he was to mock Burmann's editorial manner in the notes to his burlesque tragedy *Tom Thumb*; but it is probable that he now received his first instructions in critical theory, and began to obtain his extensive knowledge of classical literature. Certainly he was later to own a remarkable library of classical and modern texts; and his novels show that he possessed what Johnson considered the primary equipment of the modern novelist, 'learning which is to be gained from books'.

At the age of thirty-five when he began to write *Joseph Andrews*, he had had sufficient opportunity to acquire the second item in Johnson's equipment, 'experience which . . . must arise from general converse and accurate observation of the living world'. If we did not know this from *Joseph Andrews* itself, we should know it from the plays written during the seven years following his return from Leyden in 1730 and from his journalistic essays. These serve to show something of the range of that experience as well as indicating how the experience might be used by the future novelist.

Writing for the stage had taught him how to manipulate dialogue and to devise speech rhythms for distinguishing a country squire from a man-about-town or a modish lady from a young miss. It had taught him to contrive a concatenation of incidents by which the principal characters are brought together in the final scene of play or novel for the unravelling of the knot. It seems also to have accustomed him to imagine some of his scenes in terms of a drawing-room set on a stage of limited dimensions, and to offer in the novel scenes which experience told him would be effective in the theatre. His plays abound in scenes where characters are interrupted by an unexpected entry which disturbs and perplexes their existing relationship. Thus in Act III of *The Temple Beau* (1730), an early play, young Wilding is pretending to make love to Lady Lucy Pedant and has just taken her in his arms when they are interrupted by the entry first of her husband ('Hoity-toity? Hey-day! What's here to do? Have I caught you, gentlefolks. . .') and, immediately after, of Wilding's father, who has lately discovered his son's deceptions. This use of the unexpected entry is more skilfully developed in *Tom Jones* (XV, 5), in a scene where Lord Fellamar's unwanted attentions to Sophia in Lady Bellaston's house are interrupted by the entry of Squire Western, who has at last discovered where Sophia has taken refuge. Western is followed by Lady Bellaston, who joins him in representing to Sophia the advantages of agreeing to a proposal of marriage. Lord Fellamar, being assured that he was meant by Lady Bellaston and assuming that he must also be meant by Western, decides to take advantage of the new turn in the situation:

> Coming up therefore to the squire, he said, 'Though I have not the honour, sir, of being personally known to you; yet, as I find I have the happiness to have my proposals accepted, let me intercede, sir, in behalf of the young lady, that she may not be more solicited at this time.'
>
> 'You intercede, sir!' said the squire; 'why, who the devil are you?'
>
> 'Sir, I am Lord Fellamar,' answered he, 'and am the happy man, whom I hope you have done the honour of accepting for a son-in-law.'
>
> 'You are the son of a b——,' replied the squire, 'for all your laced coat. You my son-in-law, and be d——n'd to you!'
>
> 'I shall take more from you, sir, than from any man,' answered the lord; 'but I must inform you, that I am not used to hear such language without resentment.'
>
> 'Resent my a——', quoth the squire. 'Don't think I am afraid of such a fellow as thee art! because hast got a spit there dangling at thy side. Lay by your spit, and I'll give thee enough of meddling with what doth not belong to thee. I'll teach you to father-in-law me. I'll lick thy jacket.'
>
> 'It's very well, sir,' said my lord, 'I shall make no disturbance before the ladies. I am very well satisfied. Your humble servant, sir; Lady Bellaston, your most obedient.'

There can be little doubt that in this episode Fielding has made use of his theatrical experience, as he has also done in scenes involving the use of stage properties, even though the number of these is meagre. The most notable example in his plays is perhaps to be found in Act III of *The Letter Writers* (1731), where Mrs. Wisdom and her gallant Rakel are disturbed by the arrival of Mrs. Softly, and Rakel, tender of Mrs. Wisdom's reputation, hides under the table. Mrs. Softly is followed by Mr. Wisdom and a nephew, who in a drunken fit overturns the table, and discovers Rakel.

This is the prototype of more memorable discoveries, of Lady Bellaston discovering Mrs. Honour in hiding behind the bed in Jones's room (XV, 7), and of Jones discovering the philosopher Square behind a rug in Molly Seagrim's bedchamber (V, 5). It is surprising that after his early experiment in *The Letter Writers* Fielding should not have improved upon the device in a subsequent play. The hint was to be taken by Sheridan, however, who shows, in the scene of Lady Teazle's discovery behind a screen in Joseph Surface's room, that he had learned something from each of the episodes in *Tom Jones*, for he there combined both the embarrassment of Square's discovery and the reversal of fortune which sprang from Mrs. Honour's.

During his career as a dramatist Fielding had attempted a considerable number of forms. He had written witty comedies of intrigue in the Restoration manner, farces, ballad operas with political implications, burlesques, comedies reflecting upon modern manners, and satirical comedies on the pattern of Buckingham's *Rehearsal* in which an absurd play is rehearsed with comments from the author, a critical acquaintance, and the players. Two of the last of these, *Pasquin* (1736) and *The Historical Register* (1737), were amongst the most successful of his plays, and the device which he there employs of accompanying the action with critical comment from the wings may perhaps have suggested to him the 'prolegomenous' chapters of *Tom Jones* which, on a more serious level, serve the same purpose. Equally significant is his early experience of burlesque in *Tom Thumb* (1730) and *The Covent-Garden Tragedy* (1731), where by burlesquing an old-fashioned 'kind', he produced a new 'kind', as it were, by mutation. Though the burlesque of epic is not so prominent in *Joseph Andrews* and its successors as the burlesque of tragedy in *Tom Thumb*, it is by a similar process of 'mutation' that the novels arose.

Fielding's experience as a journalist was scarcely less useful to his future career than his experience in the theatre. From 1739 to 1741 he was the leader of a group of writers responsible for conducting an Opposition newspaper called *The Champion*. To this journal Fielding contributed a number of essays modelled on *The Spectator*. Just as Addison had invented a Spectator Club and had defined the *persona* of one member of the club who should write his lucubrations, aided and abetted by his fellow-members, so Fielding assumed the *persona* of Captain Hercules Vinegar, whose business it was to write about the issues of the day, aided by his wife Joan and their two sons. Like Addison, too, he varies the form of his articles, now character sketches, now lay sermons, or letters from imaginary correspondents, visions, critical papers, essays in instalments, and Saturday papers on religious matters. These essays reveal a more serious-minded Fielding than we might have supposed judging from the plays alone. Here he is to be seen formulating his views on the moral problems which form the staple of his three novels, and illustrating those problems by anecdotes and character sketches. He was also unwittingly practising himself in what was regarded as an important part of the novelist's duty. The novelist was expected to provide, in Johnson's phrase, 'lectures of conduct'. He was not merely to edify by the story he told, but to make sure that his lesson was understood. Hence the pithy, and summary comment upon manners, common alike to the novelist and the essayist.

III

For much of his future work Fielding was well prepared both in theory and in practice. It is not surprising, therefore, that from the beginning his command was assured, even though his approach was haphazard, even accidental. If it had not been for Richardson's *Pamela*, he might never have become a novelist. This story deals with a young woman's marriage outside her station in life. When a young man and a young woman of different social classes fell in love, it was generally assumed that their association could only be illegitimate. 'Why, what is all this, my

dear,' said Sir Simon Darnford, one of Richardson's characters, to his wife, 'but that our neighbour has a mind to his
mother's waiting maid! And if he takes care she wants for
nothing, I don't see any great injury will be done her. He
hurts no *family* by this.' And Parson Williams reports the
opinion of Parson Peters that this was 'too common and
fashionable a case to be withstood by a private clergyman
or two'. What made this particular case uncommon was
that Pamela resists her would-be seducer, yet cannot help
loving him in spite of his ill-treatment; and that Mr. B.
expects to be able to seduce Pamela, yet, in spite of favourable circumstances, he is won by her behaviour and against
the opinion of the world to offer her marriage.

Thus Pamela's Virtue is Rewarded. But though Richardson emphasizes that aspect of his story in his sub-title, there
is much more to the novel. Had that been all, we might
have expected that her virtue would be rewarded by
marriage in the last chapter. But the ceremony takes place
two-thirds of the way through; and yet we read on, since
it is not merely Pamela's chastity but the integrity of her
personality which is tested. She must also be shown pre-
serving in her new station her humility, her thankfulness,
her piety, and her intelligence. Hers is indeed a most
difficult task. She is required to loathe Mr. B's behaviour,
and yet to love him; to be content with her lowly position,
yet to aspire to Mr. B's hand; to be humble, yet to reprobate
aristocratic vice; to be meek, yet outspoken; to be simple,
yet quick-witted; to be innocent, yet wide-awake and on
her guard. It would seem almost impossible that Richardson
should succeed in steering so intricate a path. But each incident is related with such careful attention to detail, Pamela's
letters give so powerful a sense of immediacy, and Richardson himself preserves such an unhesitating belief in Pamela's
word and in the truth of appearances, that almost he would
persuade us to believe too. Almost, but not quite. Many contemporaries were persuaded; but others saw that a different
interpretation was possible, and amongst these was Fielding.

To convey this alternative interpretation, Fielding called upon his experience in burlesque and produced, pseudonymously, *An Apology for the Life of Mrs. Shamela Andrews. In which, the many notorious Falshoods and Misrepresentations of a book called Pamela, are Exposed and refuted; and all the matchless Arts of that young Politician, set in a true and just Light. Together with A full Account of all that passed between her and Parson Arthur Williams; whose Character is represented in a manner something different from that which he bears in Pamela. The whole being exact Copies of authentick Papers delivered to the Editor.* It is a riotous travesty, in which Pamela is shown as a shameless and designing hussy, yet ready to talk for 'a full Hour and a half, about my Vartue' or 'of honourable Designs till Supper-time', and Mr. B's full name is discovered to be Booby. And just as the rehearsed plays in *Pasquin* and *The Historical Register* had been enclosed within a framework of commentary from the supposed author and his friend, so these authentic letters are sent to Parson Tickletext, who had taken *Pamela* at Richardson's valuation, by Parson Oliver who knew the facts.

If any moral is to be drawn, it is that the distinction between being and seeming must be recognized. No exponent of the comedy of manners could fail to draw such a distinction, and Fielding's plays are especially rich in characters who are not what they seem, from Lady Gravely, the affected prude of *The Temple Beau*, to the false and grasping Valences of *The Fathers*. But Fielding had more than a professional dramatist's interest in unmasking appearances. He returned to the subject in an essay on the Pursuit of Reputation, published in *The Champion*, 4 March 1740, where he showed that folly and vice 'are continually industrious to disguise themselves', and wear the habits of virtue and wisdom; 'which the world, always judging by the outside, easily suffers them to accomplish'; and the irony of *The Life of Mr. Jonathan Wild the Great* is sustained—tediously, it must be admitted—to prove that the Great Man, properly considered, is no better than a gangster.

The distinction between being and seeming is the guiding principle of *Joseph Andrews*. In the preface to his novel Fielding explains that the Ridiculous is his province, that the only source of the true Ridiculous is Affectation, and that Affectation 'proceeds from one of these two causes, Vanity or Hypocrisy'. To display the Ridiculous he has devised this new kind of writing, the comic epic poem in prose, observing the best epic practice in such matters as fable and characters; but whereas the epic fable is customarily grave and solemn, his will be light and ridiculous, and whereas epic characters are of the highest, his will mostly be of inferior rank and manners. The difficulty is to see how Fielding interprets the representation of the fable in action. Fortunately he is more explicit in the preface he wrote for his sister's novel, *David Simple* (1744). There, after referring to his preface to *Joseph Andrews*, he mentions the two great originals of all epic writing, the *Iliad* and the *Odyssey*, which:

> differ principally in the action, which in the *Iliad* is entire and uniform; in the *Odyssey*, is rather a series of actions, all tending to produce one great end.

The followers of Homer have all observed this principal difference, whether their imitations were serious or comic; and so we see that just as Pope in *The Dunciad* fixed on one action, Butler and Cervantes fixed on a series. His sister's work belongs to the latter category:

> the fable consists of a series of separate adventures, detached from and independent on each other, yet all tending to one great end.

The same may also be seen in *Joseph Andrews*. That also is an Odyssean epic, 'consisting of a series of separate adventures, detached from and independent of each other, yet all tending to one great end'; and it may be observed that just as the *Odyssey* relates the adventures of Odysseus in finding his way home and the hardships which befell him after incurring the wrath of Poseidon, so Fielding relates the adventures of Joseph Andrews and Parson Adams in finding their way home and the hardships which befell them after

Joseph had incurred the wrath of Lady Booby. Perhaps contemporary readers might have noticed an even closer application of the burlesque. The critic Ramsay had pointed out that in Fénelon's *Aventures de Télémaque* it is the hatred of Venus rather than the wrath of Poseidon that supplies the cause of the action, and that 'the Hatred of *Venus* against a young Prince, that despises Pleasure for the Sake of Virtue, and subdues his Passions by the Assistance of Wisdom, is a Fable drawn from Nature, and at the same Time includes the sublimest Morality'. No reader could fail to relish the notion of the lascivious Lady Booby in the role of Venus, whose desire for her handsome footman Joseph Andrews is turned to hatred when that Young Prince despises Pleasure for the sake of Virtue, and subdues his passions by the assistance of his sister Pamela's wisdom.

But what is the great end to which all the separate adventures are tending? Why, surely, the display of the Ridiculous, of those affectations which arise from vanity and hypocrisy. This is the characteristic common to Lady Booby, Mrs. Slipslop, and Mrs. Grave-airs, all of them women who pretend to more modesty, more learning, or more gentility than they possess. And this is the characteristic of the innkeepers and their wives who can make a show of human kindness once they are satisfied of the standing of their guests, of the soldiers who pretend to valour, of the justices who pretend to a knowledge of the law, and of the parsons who pretend to godliness. Even Parson Trulliber can make a show of Methodism, when he is satisfied that Adams has not come to buy his pigs: 'Get out of my doors', he cries, when Adams tells him that, in addition to faith, he must perform the good works of giving to the needy; 'Fellow, dost thou speak against faith in my house? I will no longer remain under the same roof with a wretch who speaks wantonly of faith and the Scriptures.'

The two interpolated stories fall into place in this pattern. The Unfortunate Jilt is a story of pretence to affection, and the story of Mr. Wilson is a tale of the pretences practised

in London life. Vanity of vanities is Mr. Wilson's theme as
he recalls his experiences of life in the Temple amongst smart
fellows who drank with lords they did not know and in-
trigued with women they never saw; and of town coquettes
animated solely by vanity who sometimes have a whim to
affect wisdom, wit, good-nature, politeness, and health, but
are also affected to put on ugliness, folly, nonsense, ill-
nature, ill-breeding, and sickness in their turns.

Such are Mr. Wilson's reflexions. Far from being an idle
digression, they are highly appropriate to Fielding's scheme
and purpose; for his action, by confining him to the high
road and the inn, precludes him from commenting upon
London life, and it is a sample of London society which
Mr. Wilson's story exposes.

But these at worst are transient characters, and at best
they are minor. What of Parson Adams himself? He too
has his vanities, innocent vanities indeed, of his learning and
his power as a preacher. His role however is that of a modern
Don Quixote; a man of good sense, good parts, and good
nature, as Fielding declares, but 'as entirely ignorant of the
ways of this world as an infant just entered into it could
possibly be'. His book-reading did not, like his illustrious
prototype's, lead him to mistake windmills for giants or inns
for castles; it led him instead to expect on every hand an
honest, undesigning, Christian behaviour. He is therefore
constantly the victim of deceit. But he never loses our affection, partly because his expectations are noble, and partly
because (like Don Quixote again) he hurls himself upon the
oppressor thinking only of the blows his two fists or his
crabstick will deliver, and nothing of those he will receive.
It is not merely in such episodes as the fight at the inn which
interrupts the story of The Unfortunate Jilt, or the 'roasting'
of Adams by the fox-hunting squire (which recalls the treatment of Don Quixote at the hands of the Duke and
Duchess), or the midnight tussle with Mrs. Slipslop where
Adams believes himself bewitched, that the reader recognizes the justice of the assertion on the title-page of *Joseph*

Andrews, that it is 'Written in Imitation of the Manner of Cervantes'.

But there are two sides to the relationship of being and seeming. While most of the men and women we meet in *Joseph Andrews* are worse than they seem, others are better. And though the bedraggled appearance of the worthy Adams is the most prominent example, Fielding asks us to notice that the man who pays the stranded travellers' bill is not the wealthy Parson Trulliber but 'a fellow who had been formerly a drummer in an Irish regiment, and now travelled the country as a pedlar'; that when Joseph lies sick at the Tow-wouses' inn, it is not the surgeon, or the parson, or the innkeeper, who looks after him, but Betty the chambermaid, whose morals are no better than they should be; and when Joseph has been found wounded and naked in a ditch, it is not any of the fine ladies in a passing coach who takes pity on him, but the postilion:

> (a lad who hath been since transported for robbing a hen-roost), [who] voluntarily stript off a greatcoat, his only garment, at the same time swearing a great oath (for which he was rebuked by the passengers), 'that he would rather ride in his shirt all his life than suffer a fellow-creature to lie in so miserable a condition'.

To some extent, this anatomy of the ridiculous is a counterblast to *Pamela*, and by recalling certain incidents in that novel and introducing one or two of its characters, Fielding made sure that we should keep *Pamela* in view. Richardson had placed an implicit trust in the truth of appearances. But that way lies self-deception: it is only by the most careful scrutiny that we can see beneath appearances and find the true springs of human action.

IV

Yet appearances are important too. 'It is not enough', Fielding writes, 'that your designs, nay that your actions, are intrinsically good; you must take care that they shall appear so'; for 'prudence and circumspection are necessary even to the best of men'. The passage occurs in one of those chapters of *Tom Jones* (III, 7) 'in which the author himself makes his appearance on the stage', and it is close to the heart of the novel. The theme is in fact announced in similar terms in the Dedication:

> I have endeavoured strongly to inculcate, that virtue and innocence can scarce ever be injured but by indiscretion; and . . . it is this alone which often betrays them into the snares which deceit and villany spread for them.

To illustrate this Fielding chose a hero as typical of his order of society as the epic hero was of his. We are asked to recognize that Tom, in spite of some lack of prudence and circumspection, and in spite of some contraventions of the moral code, is essentially a good man. It might be said of Tom as Ramsay had said of Fénelon's Telemachus:

> Our Poet does not lift *Telemachus* above Humanity; he makes him fall into such Weaknesses, as are compatible with a sincere Love of Virtue.

Young Mr. Blifil, on the other hand, with whom Tom is brought up in Mr. Allworthy's household, has more than enough of prudence and circumspection, but his love of virtue is on a par with the affectations which Fielding exposed in *Joseph Andrews*. The distinction is one which Sheridan was to familiarize when he contrasted the brothers Charles and Joseph Surface in *The School for Scandal*.

The best critical theory of the day was agreed that an epic should have a beginning, a middle, and an end, that the beginning should deal with the causes of the action, and that in the causes might be observed two opposite 'designs', the hero's and the design of those who opposed him. In adopting these sensible precepts, Fielding provided an introductory section of six books in which numerous incidents open Tom's character and reveal the designs of Blifil and his two tutors, Thwackum and Square, who sought to prejudice Tom in the eyes of Mr. Allworthy and to prevent him from marrying Sophia and inheriting Squire Western's estate. Tom is shown (IV, 6) to have 'somewhat about him, which, though I think writers are not thoroughly agreed in its name' (the philosopher Shaftesbury had called it the 'moral sense')

> . . . doth certainly inhabit some human breasts; whose use is not so properly to distinguish right from wrong, as to prompt and incite them to the former, and to restrain and withhold them from the latter. . . . Though he did not always act rightly, yet he never did otherwise without feeling and suffering for it

Thus the boy is incited to sell the little horse which Mr. Allworthy had given him so as to prevent the family of a dismissed servant from starving, and he is prompted to risk his neck in recovering Sophia's pet bird which Blifil had maliciously allowed to escape. And if as a young man he is also prompted to fornication with the gamekeeper's daughter, he is prepared to deal honourably with her until he discovers that he was not the first to seduce her; and if he was drunk and disorderly in Mr. Allworthy's house, it was because he had already been thrown into an 'immoderate excess of rapture' on hearing that Mr. Allworthy was recovering from his dangerous illness. Allworthy summarizes (V, 7) what Fielding wishes us to think of Tom, when he says to him on his sickbed:

> I am convinced, my child, that you have much goodness, generosity, and honour, in your temper: if you will add prudence and religion to these, you must be happy.

But in spite of his conviction, Allworthy allows his mind to be poisoned by the malicious insinuations of Blifil, and turns Tom away from his house into a series of adventures on the high road, corresponding to those of Joseph Andrews and Parson Adams. They fill the second six books of the novel and correspond, in epic terms, to 'the Shipping off of Æneas, his Voyages, his Battels, and all the Obstacles he met with', which (in the words of Le Bossu, the chief authority on epic structure at that time) 'compose a just Middle; [for]

they are a Consequence of the Destruction of Troy . . . and these same Incidents require an End'.

The high road led to London, and on it are not only Tom (and Partridge, his Sancho Panza) but Sophia, who has fled from her father's house to escape being forced into marriage with Blifil. As in *Joseph Andrews*, the high road and the inn provide a suitable scene for the testing of character, the recognition of bad nature masquerading as good, and of good nature concealed or tainted by imprudence. Tom has something to learn even from the Man of the Hill who, like Mr. Wilson and like many a character in epic, is permitted to interrupt the narrative with his story. The Man of the Hill provides further instances of imprudence, in particular of incautiousness in placing his affections, and as a result he had become a misanthrope and a hermit. But, as Tom permits himself to comment (VIII, 15), 'What better could be expected in love derived from the stews, or in friendship first produced and nourished at the gaming table?' One must not think evil of the rest of mankind on that account, for, as Tom continues, enunciating Fielding's doctrines of the Good-Natured Man and the deceptiveness of appearances:

> If there was, indeed, much more wickedness in the world than there is, it would not prove such general assertions against human nature, since much of this arrives by mere accident, and many a man who commits evil is not totally bad and corrupt in his heart.

Sophia too is learning as much as Tom, directly in such scenes as that at the inn at Upton, and by proxy as she listens to Mrs. Fitzpatrick's cautionary tale of her imprudent marriage, interrupted as it is by appeals to Sophia to declare how she would have acted in like circumstances.

The lovers reach London independently and the final section of six further books begins. Tom's good nature is as clear as ever, notably in his generous treatment of the highwayman who was driven by penury to attack him, and in his chivalrous championship of Mrs. Miller's daughter; but alas, his imprudence is clearer still in 'the ignominious

circumstance of being kept' by Lady Bellaston. Fielding
never asks his readers to overlook Tom's misdemeanours. His
worst offence is most severely punished, for his relations
with Lady Bellaston cannot be forgiven by Sophia; and we
see him at the end of the Sixteenth Book at the nadir of his
fortunes, rejected by Sophia, dismissed from Allworthy's
favour, and imprisoned on a charge of murdering his opponent in a duel. 'Such', Fielding muses (XVII, 1), 'are the
calamities in which he is at present involved, owing to his
imprudence . . . that we almost despair of bringing him to
any good; and if our reader delights in seeing executions, I
think he ought not to lose any time in taking a first row at
Tyburn.' Readers of the epic will recognize that the time is
ripe for a Discovery or a Reversal of Fortune, perhaps even
for both, and they will recall that it was not unusual for the
author to invoke divine aid for rescuing a hero in distress.
Fielding has prepared both for his Discovery—that was
allowed for in making Tom a foundling—and for his
Reversal of Fortune; but he disdains to employ the marvellous. It is true that luck is on Tom's side when his victim in
the duel recovers from his wound, and when the facts of his
parentage (concealed by Blifil) are discovered; but in other
respects the reader is asked to recognize that Tom has
worked his passage. He has cast his bread upon the waters
in acts of abundant good nature, and by the assistance of
Mrs. Miller's representations to Mr. Allworthy he finds it
after many days. His Virtue is Rewarded by restoration into
the favour of Allworthy and the good graces of Sophia.
Since he is now discovered to be Allworthy's nephew and
heir, Squire Western has no further objections to bestowing
his daughter upon him; they marry, and 'preserve the
purest and tenderest affection for each other, an affection
daily increased and confirmed by mutual endearments, and
mutual esteem'.

This is a pious hope which the reader may find it difficult
to share, for it rests upon the large assumption that Tom had
ceased to be indiscreet. Furthermore he was at best a good-

natured man; and though endowed with a well-developed Moral Sense, he required on Allworthy's evidence to add religion as well as prudence to his good nature. Even if we allow that he had become prudent, there is nothing to show that he had become religious. Some such reflexions seem to have occurred to Fielding, for his next novel, *Amelia* (1752), begins where *Tom Jones* leaves off. Captain and Mrs. Booth also entertained the purest and tenderest affection for each other and confirmed it by mutual endearments and mutual esteem, yet various accidents befell them owing partly to Booth's character, and it is with these accidents and with their effect upon this worthy couple that the novel is concerned.

V

The decision to deal with the accidents of domestic life set Fielding some new problems in structure. The high road and the inn could have no place here since married folk are not usually nomadic, and consequently we miss the Odyssean–Quixotic episodes which provided him in the earlier novels with so many shining opportunities for unmasking affectation and testing character. He had also to decide how to relate the earlier history of his couple, a problem he had not been required to face before. But the comic adaptation of epic conventions was ready to hand here as it had been at the beginning of *Joseph Andrews*. Just as Æneas was stranded on the coasts of Carthage, was succoured there by Dido, related to her his story, and consummated his furtive love in a cave, so Captain Booth was stranded in Newgate Prison, was succoured there by Miss Matthews, a high-class courtesan, related to her his story, and consummated his furtive love in a superior kind of cell. Nor is this merely an ingenious piece of burlesque. Booth's misdemeanour with Miss Matthews, which he is ashamed to confess to Amelia, dogs him throughout the novel; while the sombreness of the opening scenes in Newgate Prison set the tone of the book. Fielding takes care to show us the squalor and oppression which is the lot of the penniless prisoner, and on the other hand the relative comfort which is to be had at the price of a bribe; and he describes the coarse and depraved ruffians, male and female, the tricksters and sharpers, who molest and prey upon the weak, the unfortunate, and even the innocent, who have come there through a miscarriage of justice. This is the scene in which we first discover Booth, whose previous history shows him to be imprudent, liable to deception, with 'very slight and uncertain' notions of religion, yet essentially good-natured. He will not return to Newgate, but he will always be in danger of return. And when he escapes, the reader recognizes that Newgate was only a somewhat more lurid epitome of society outside, where merit counts for nothing, where civil and military places go by influence exerted for a bribe, where those in high place have rogues, pimps, and bawds in their pay, and where gallantry is a cover for fornication and adultery. Fielding had said as much long ago in his play *The Modern Husband* (1731), and had repeated it in *Jonathan Wild*; and if *Joseph Andrews* and *Tom Jones* appear lighter in tone than *Amelia*, it is only because the scene is laid more frequently in the country. London is the breeding-place for such creatures as Lord Fellamar and Lady Bellaston, and Mr. Wilson anticipated Booth in finding that in London 'poverty and distress, with their horrid trains of duns, attorneys, bailiffs, haunted me day and night. My clothes grew shabby, my credit bad, my friends and acquaintance of all kinds cold'.

The scene is in fact so sombre that a tragic conclusion seems inevitable. Even a stronger and a better man than Booth could scarcely escape that fate. In considering the conclusion to which he was leading his 'worthy couple', Fielding is likely to have paid attention to the best critical teaching available. The consensus of opinion amongst commentators upon the epic pointed to a conclusion favourable to the hero. Le Bossu indeed could discover no reason why that should be so:

'yet if any heed be given to Authority,' he concluded, 'I do not know any one Instance of a Poet, who finishes his Piece with the Misfortunes of his Heroe. . . . The *Epick Poem's* Action is of a larger Extent than that of the Theatre; [and] it would perhaps be less satisfactory to the Reader, if, after so much Pains and so long Troubles with which this kind of Poem is always fill'd, it should at last bring them to a doleful and unhappy End.'

The easiest way of bringing the Booths to a happy end might well have been to repeat the formula of *Tom Jones* and show the eventual reward of the hero's virtuous actions. But Fielding seems to have been no longer content with such teaching. It was Booth's mistake to believe that as men 'act entirely from their passions, their actions can have neither merit or demerit'. If a man's ruling passion happened to be benevolence, he would relieve the distress of others; but if it were avarice, ambition, or pride, other men's miseries would have no effect upon him. Booth is eventually to be corrected of an error, which to Amelia seemed little better than atheism, by reading a volume of Barrow's sermons while detained in the bailiff's house; but in the meanwhile Fielding allows him little opportunity for charity. The reader notices instead how his imprudence in the use of what little money he has reduces Amelia to penury, and how his ill-placed trust and his single act of fornication endangers her chastity. She, however, shows herself to be on all occasions a model of wifely prudence, constancy, obedience, forgiveness, and love.

'To retrieve the ill consequences of a foolish conduct, and by struggling manfully with distress to subdue it, is one of the noblest efforts of wisdom and virtue.' That is all that Fielding asks of his worthy couple; and having displayed their struggles, he is not averse to rescuing them by an Epic Discovery (that Amelia is an heiress) and an Epic Reversal of Fortune, which enables a now prudent and Christian Booth to retire to a country estate.

In *Amelia*, as in *Tom Jones*, Fielding infers that at the end of the book the hero is in some respects an altered man without persuading us of the fact. Dickens was the first novelist to succeed in such persuasion and George Eliot the first to specialize in showing the modifying effect of incident upon character. These Victorian successes have made demands which the modern reader is inclined to impose both upon earlier novelists and earlier dramatists without perhaps reflecting whether changes in character are altogether necessary or always important. *Amelia*, like *Tom Jones*, deals with wider issues than the modification of character. It has to do not merely with Booth and his wife, but with miseries and distresses typical of mid-eighteenth century London life. No other novel provides such a wide panorama of London society or better conveys what it was like to live in London in the seventeen-fifties.

VI

In a paper which he wrote for the last of his periodicals, *The Covent Garden Journal* (28 January 1752), Fielding declared that he would not trouble the world with any more novels. He had not been entirely committed to the profession of letters since the abrupt termination of his dramatic career. The severity of his attack upon Walpole's government in *Pasquin* had led directly to the Licensing Act of 1737 and to the closure of all theatres but Drury Lane and Covent Garden. Fielding's Little Theatre in the Haymarket was the principal victim, and his chief source of income was thus removed. He thereupon began a serious study of the law, was called to the bar in 1740, and practised for some time on the Western Circuit. Shortly after completing *Tom Jones* in 1748, and before its publication, he had been appointed a police-court magistrate at Bow Street, and his jurisdiction was soon extended to the whole of the County of Middlesex. As a magistrate he was exceptionally industrious, and did much to break up the gangs of thieves which infested London. His *Enquiry Into the Causes of the late Increase of Robbers* (1751), dedicated to Lord Chancellor Hardwicke, shows both an extensive knowledge of the law and an intimate acquaintance with the evil and its origin. His energies might have been directed more and more to clearing up the criminal underworld if his health had not broken down. In the summer of 1754 he undertook a sea trip to Lisbon with his wife and daughter in a desperate search for health, and whiled away his time in keeping a diary. This he revised, and the manuscript was posthumously published as *A Journal of a Voyage to Lisbon*. Not the least of its merits is the picture it gives us of the man himself, affectionately considerate to his family, patiently suffering from an incurable disease, yet observing with undiminished zest the oddities of human behaviour, and seizing such opportunities as incidents offered for social or political comment. The book is prefaced by a disquisition on travel literature comparable in kind to the disquisition on the comic epic poem in prose which prefaces *Joseph Andrews*. Once again Fielding declared that he was laying down the rules for a kind of writing which had not been properly undertaken before (except by Lord Anson in the published account of his circumnavigation, 1740–44); for travellers seem to have fallen either into the fault of 'filling their pages with monsters which nobody hath ever seen, and with adventures which never have, nor could possibly have happened to them', or on the other hand they:

> waste their time and paper with recording things and facts of so common a kind, that they challenge no other right of being remembered than as they had the honour of having happened to the author.

This opportunity of reforming travel literature was as haphazard as the chance he took of reforming the novel, but even if he had lived longer—he died on 8 October 1754 at the age of forty-seven—it was not likely that he would have had occasion to write more in this kind. It is easy, however, to see that his theories might have been profitably applied to biography, and that he was well equipped by imagination, a reverence for truth, judgement, and a sense of proportion to succeed in that kindred form.

But this is idle speculation. Even though he may have felt that he had outgrown the novel, it is there that his achievement lies; and it is an achievement typical of an age which relished the mock-epics of Pope and the ballad operas of Gay. Like those poets Fielding brought literary experience gained in other writing and a wealth of critical learning to bear upon the production of a new form, but a form which constantly recalls older, well-tried forms and adapts them to the spirit and use of his own times; and he used this form to display 'just copies of human manners' and to offer 'lectures of conduct, and introductions into life'.

HENRY FIELDING

Select Bibliography

BIBLIOGRAPHIES

CORDASCO, F. *Henry Fielding: A List of Critical Studies Published from 1895-1946*. Brooklyn: Long Island University Press, 1948.

There are long bibliographies in Wilbur C. Cross, *The History of Henry Fielding*, and F. Homes Dudden, *Henry Fielding*—see below.

COLLECTED EDITIONS

The Works. Edited by Arthur Murphy. 4 vols. London: Millar, 1762.

The Dramatic Works. 4 vols. London: Strahan, 1783.

The Works. Edited by Alexander Chalmers. 10 vols. London: Johnson, 1806.

The Works. Edited by Thomas Roscoe. London: Washbourne, 1840.

The Works. Edited by Leslie Stephen. 10 vols. London: Smith, Elder, 1882.

The Works. Edited by George Saintsbury. 12 vols. London: Dent, 1893.

The Works. Edited by Edmund Gosse. 12 vols. New York: Scribner's, 1899.

The Complete Works. Edited by W. E. Henley and others. 16 vols. New York: Croscup and Sterling, 1903.

The Works. Edited by G. H. Maynardier. 12 vols. New York: Sproul, 1903.

Fielding's Novels. Shakespeare Head Edition. 10 vols. Oxford: Blackwell, 1926.

SELECTIONS

Miscellanies. 3 vols. London: Millar, 1743.

The Beauties of Fielding. London: Kearsley, 1782.

Miscellanies and Poems. Edited by James P. Browne. Boston: Little, Brown, 1872.

Selected Essays. Edited by Gordon Hall Gerould. New York: Ginn, 1905.

Fielding. Edited by George Saintsbury. London: Bell, 1909.

Fielding. Edited by L. Rice-Oxley. Oxford: Clarendon Press, 1923.

SEPARATE WORKS

NOVELS

Note. Dates of original London publication are given. Modern editions and paperbacks are also recorded here.

The History of the Adventures of Joseph Andrews and of His Friend Mr. Abraham Adams. 2 vols. 1742.

Preface by George Saintsbury (Everyman's Library); preface by L. Rice-Oxley (The World's Classics); Modern Library Paperback; Norton Paperback; edited together with *Shamela* by M. D. Battestin (Riverside Edition).

The Life of Mr. Jonathan Wild the Great, 1743.

First published in *Miscellanies*. A new edition with considerable corrections and additions, 1754. The World's Classics edition reprints the text of 1743 with the variants of 1754 in an appendix; Signet Paperback; with the *Journal of a Voyage to Lisbon*, Everyman's Library.

The History of Tom Jones, A Foundling. 6 vols. 1749.

Introduction by George Saintsbury (Everyman's Library); Modern Library Paperback; Vintage Paperback.

Amelia. 4 vols. 1752.

Fielding's revised text was first published in Murphy's edition of the *Works*. Introduction by George Saintsbury (Everyman's Library); Dolphin Paperback.

PLAYS

Note. Dates of original London production or publication are given. Modern editions are also recorded here.

Love in Several Masques, A Comedy, 1728.

The Temple Beau, A Comedy, 1730.

The Author's Farce, 1730.

Tom Thumb, A Tragedy, 1730.

A revised edition with annotations, entitled *The Tragedy of Tragedies; or the Life and Death of Tom Thumb the Great*, was published in 1731. Both texts are reprinted in J. T. Hilhouse's edition (New Haven: Yale University Press, 1918).

Rape Upon Rape; Or, The Justice Caught In His Own Trap, A Comedy, 1730.

The Letter-Writers: Or, A New Way to Keep a Wife At Home, A Farce,
1731.

The Welsh Opera: Or, The Grey Mare the Better Horse, 1731.

The Lottery, A Farce, 1732.

The Modern Husband, A Comedy, 1732.

The Old Debauchees, A Comedy, 1732.

The Covent-Garden Tragedy, 1732.

*The Mock Doctor, Or, The Dumb Lady Cur'd. A Comedy, Done From
Molière,* 1732.

The Miser. A Comedy, Taken From Plautus and Molière, 1733.

The Intriguing Chambermaid, A Comedy, 1734.

Don Quixote In England, A Comedy, 1734.

Contains the famous songs "When Mighty roast beef was the Englishman's food" and "The dusky night rides down the sky."

An Old Man Taught Wisdom: Or, The Virgin Unmask'd, A Farce, 1735.

The Universal Gallant: Or, The Different Husbands, A Comedy, 1735.

Pasquin, A Dramatick Satire on the Times, 1736.

Tumble-Down Dick: Or, Phaeton in the Suds. A Dramatick Entertainment,
1736.

Eurydice, A Farce, 1737.

The Historical Register for the Year 1736, 1737.

Also contains *Eurydice Hiss'd,* "a very merry Tragedy."

Miss Lucy in Town, A Farce, 1742.

The Wedding-Day, A Comedy, 1743.

The Fathers: Or, The Good-Natur'd Man, A Comedy, 1778.

OTHER WRITINGS

Note. Dates of original London publication are given. Modern
editions are also recorded here.

The Champion, November 15, 1739–June 19, 1740; 2 vols., 1741.

Of True Greatness, 1741.

The Vernoniad, 1741.

An Apology for the Life of Mrs. Shamela Andrews, 1741.

Edited by R. B. Johnson (Berkshire: The Golden Cockerel Press,
1926); by Brian W. Downs (Cambridge: Heffer, 1932); by Sheridan
W. Baker, Jr. (Berkeley: University of California Press, 1953); by
Ian Watt (Augustan Facsimile Society, 1956); and, with *Joseph Andrews,*
by M. Battestin (Riverside Paperback).

The Crisis, A Sermon, 1741.

The Opposition, A Vision, 1742.

A Full Vindication of the Dutchess Dowager of Marlborough, 1742.

Plutus, The God of Riches, A Comedy, Translated From the Original Greek of Aristophanes, 1742.

Some Papers Proper to be Read Before the Royal Society, 1743.

A Serious Address to the People of Great Britain, 1745.

A Dialogue Between the Devil, the Pope, and the Pretender, 1745.

The True Patriot, November 5, 1745–June 17, 1746.

Ovid's Art of Love Paraphrased, 1747.

 Edited by C. E. Jones (Augustan Reprint Society, 1961).

The Jacobite's Journal, December 5, 1747–November 5, 1748.

A Charge Delivered to the Grand Jury, 1749.

A True State of the Case of Bosavern Penlez, 1749.

An Enquiry into the Causes of the Late Increase of Robbers, 1751.

A Plan of the Universal Register Office, 1752.

The Covent-Garden Journal, January 4–November 25, 1752.

 Edited by G. E. Jensen (2 vols. New Haven: Yale University Press, 1915).

Examples of the Interposition of Providence in the Detection and Punishment of Murder, 1752.

A Proposal for Making an Effectual Provision for the Poor, 1753.

A Clear State of the Case of Elizabeth Canning, 1753.

The Journal of a Voyage to Lisbon, 1755.

 A full edition was published the same year and suppressed. Edited by Austin Dobson (London: Chiswick Press, 1892); by J. H. Lobban (Cambridge: University Press, 1913); with *Jonathan Wild* (Everyman's Library); edited by H. E. Pagliaro (New York: Nardon Press, 1963).

"A New Letter from Fielding." By E. L. McAdam. *Yale Review*, Vol. XXXVIII (1949).

 A remarkable commendation of *Clarissa* addressed to Richardson.

BIOGRAPHICAL AND CRITICAL STUDIES

DOBSON, AUSTIN. *Fielding*. London: Macmillan, 1883.

GODDEN, G. M. *Henry Fielding: A Memoir*. London: Low, 1910.

CROSS, WILBUR L. *The History of Henry Fielding*. 3 vols. New Haven: Yale University Press, 1910.

 The standard biography, with valuable bibliography.

DIGEON, AURÉLIEN. *The Novels of Fielding.* London: Routledge, 1925.

BLANCHARD, FREDERIC T. *Fielding the Novelist.* New Haven: Yale University Press, 1926.
A study of Fielding's reputation.

BATESON, F. W. *English Comic Drama 1700–1750.* Oxford: Clarendon Press, 1929.

THORNBURY, ETHEL M. *Henry Fielding's Theory of the Comic Prose Epic.* Madison: University of Wisconsin Studies in Language and Literature No. 30, 1931.

BISSELL, FREDERICK O. *Fielding's Theory of the Novel.* Ithaca: Cornell University Press, 1933.

JONES, BENJAMIN M. *Henry Fielding, Novelist and Magistrate.* London: Allen and Unwin, 1933.

SHERBURN, GEORGE. "Fielding's Amelia: An Interpretation," *ELH,* Vol. III (1936).
An outstanding essay.

IRWIN, WILLIAM R. *The Making of Jonathan Wild.* New York: Columbia University Press, 1941.

WILLCOCKS, M. P. *A True Born Englishman: Being the Life of Henry Fielding.* London: Allen and Unwin, 1947.

JENKINS, ELIZABETH. *Henry Fielding.* Denver: Swallow, 1948.

DUDDEN, F. HOMES. *Henry Fielding: His Life, Works, and Times.* 2 vols. Oxford: Clarendon Press, 1952.
Useful on the social background.

CRANE, R. S. "The Concept of Plot and the Plot of Tom Jones," *Critics and Criticism Ancient and Modern.* Edited by R. S. Crane. Chicago: University of Chicago Press, 1952.

MURRY, J. MIDDLETON. *Unprofessional Essays.* London: Cape, 1956.
Contains a masterly defense against some modern denigration.

BATTESTIN, M. C. *The Moral Basis of Fielding's Art.* Middletown, Conn.: Wesleyan University Press, 1959.

MILLER, HENRY K. *Essays on Fielding's Miscellanies.* Princeton: Princeton University Press, 1961.

JOHNSON, MAURICE. *Fielding's Art of Fiction.* Philadelphia: University of Pennsylvania Press, 1961.

PAULSON, RONALD, ed. *Fielding: A Collection of Critical Essays.* Englewood Cliffs, N. J.: Prentice Hall, 1962.

LAURENCE STERNE

by D. W. Jefferson

LAURENCE STERNE
From a painting by an unidentified artist
in the National Portrait Gallery, London

LAURENCE STERNE was born at Clonmel, Tipperary, Ireland, on November 24, 1713. He died in London on March 8, 1768.

LAURENCE STERNE

I

IN MORE than one place Laurence Sterne claims a medicinal value for his great comic masterpiece *Tristram Shandy*:

> —If 'tis wrote against anything,—'tis wrote, an' please your worships, against the spleen! in order, by a more frequent and a more convulsive elevation and depression of the diaphragm, and the succussations of the intercostal and abdominal muscles in laughter, to drive the *gall* and other *bitter juices* from the gall-bladder, liver, and sweet-bread of his majesty's subjects, with all the inimicitious passions which belong to them, down into their duodenums.

In another passage he writes:

> True Shandeism, think what you will against it, opens the heart and lungs, and like all those affections which partake of its nature, it forces the blood and other vital fluids of the body to run freely through its channels, makes the wheel of life run long and cheerfully round.

But turning from *Tristram Shandy* to a letter written to his amiable companion, John Hall-Stevenson, in which he complains of 'a thin death-doing pestiferous north-east wind' blowing upon him, we see the virtues of the Shandean philosophy in another light:

> . . . and if God . . . had not poured forth the spirit of Shandeism into me, which will not suffer me to think two minutes upon any grave subject, I would else just now lay down and die. . . .

Sterne was long a sick man, a victim to hæmorrhages of the lungs, driven to travel abroad for his health. The gaiety of *Tristram Shandy* and also of *A Sentimental Journey* takes on a different significance against this background.

Sterne's character is of a kind which needs, but which also inspires, tender and careful handling. No reputation has suffered more than his from nineteenth-century moral prejudice and obtuseness: Thackeray's account of him in *The English Humorists of the Eighteenth Century* is one of the disgraces of English criticism. Our own age can perhaps more easily accept simply as psychological fact some aspects of his life which gave scandal to the Victorians. He was emotionally unstable. His marriage with Elizabeth Lumley was not very successful: she has been described as a 'fretful porcupine', and no doubt there were faults on his side. After eighteen years of married life she had a curious mental breakdown, and it was after this that Sterne's helpless susceptibility manifested itself in a series of sentimental relationships (they were not affairs of physical passion) which are not quite in keeping with the character of a clergyman. He was singularly unabashed about this side of his nature, as the following passage from a letter testifies:

> . . . I am glad that you are in love—'twill cure you (at least) of the spleen, which has a bad effect on both man and woman— I myself must ever have some dulcinea in my head—it harmonizes the soul—and in those cases I first endeavour to make the lady believe so, or rather I begin first to make myself believe that I am in love—but I carry on my affairs quite in the French way, sentimentally—'*l'amour*' (they say) '*n'est rien sans sentiment*'.

What the modern reader may find engaging here is Sterne's easy candour. Perhaps it is easier to-day to sympathize with an aspect of him which has tended in the past to alienate sympathy; namely, the elements of artifice which accompanies his expressions of emotion. Even in the *Journal to Eliza*, written to the woman who meant much more to him than any of the others, and during a period of overwrought emotion combined with poor health, he shows an artist's awareness of the exquisite distress he is depicting:

> Ap. 28. I was not deceived, Eliza! by my presentiment that I should find thee out in my dreams; for I have been with thee almost the whole night, alternatively soothing Thee, or telling thee my sorrows—I have rose up comforted & strengthened,— & found myself so much better, that I ordered my Carriage, to carry me to our mutual friend—Tears ran down her cheeks when

she saw how pale & wan I was—never gentle creature sym-
pathized more tenderly—I beseech you, cried the good Soul, not
to regard either difficulties or expences, but to fly to Eliza directly
—I see you will dye without her—save yourself for her—How
shall I look her in the face? What can I say to her, when on her
return I have to tell her, That her Yorick is no more!—Tell her
my dear friend, said I, that I will meet her in a better world— &
that I have left this, because I could not live without her; tell
Eliza, my dear friend, added I—That I died broken hearted—and
that you were a witness to it—as I said this she burst into the
most pathetick flood of Tears that ever kindly Nature shed—
you never beheld so affecting a scene—'twas too much for
Nature! . . .

Upon our response to this depends very largely our response to Sterne as a man. To some readers it is sheer wanton
indulgence, self-conscious manipulation of the feelings, and
fundamentally insincere. But perhaps it is wiser to recognize that everyone has his 'style', in the emotions as in
other things. To the present writer, at least, the *Journal to
Eliza* is a moving document, the record of genuine suffering.
If Sterne was, to use an unkind modern term, somewhat
exhibitionist about his feelings, these outpourings with all
their elements of conscious heightening are the expression
of a need. There is, of course, pathological weakness here,
and it must be related to his state of physical health. But it
was Sterne's gift that he could make something out of his
weaknesses. He expressed himself to the full, and somehow
the result is humanly acceptable. Recent scholarship has
uncovered some much less attractive cases of emotional
instability among the Victorian writers; Thackeray himself
was somewhat frustrated and unfulfilled, which may help to
explain his dislike of Sterne's freedom and fluency in
matters of the heart.

We might feel less kindly about this side of Sterne's life
were it not for the agreeable impression we get from his
letters and from outside testimony of his efforts during these
later years to make things as comfortable as possible for his

wife. The solicitous interest he took in the details of her journey to France when she decided to join him there with their daughter Lydia; his patience with her trying humours during their sojourn there; and his reasonable attitude to her financial demands, after he had returned to his Yorkshire parish and she had formed the project of living apart from him; all this testifies to good elements in him and to a sweetness of disposition in the face of vexation. How far he is to be blamed for the central fact of the failure of their marriage is a matter concerning which we have insufficient evidence.

Our own age is not only better equipped temperamentally to appreciate Sterne and his work; it also has the advantage of more information about his life, for which we are indebted partly to a nineteenth-century biographer, Percy Fitzgerald, but more especially to an American scholar, Wilbur L. Cross, whose monumental *Life and Times of Laurence Sterne* (1925) destroyed a number of malicious traditions which misled earlier critics. We now have more evidence, for example, about his treatment of his mother, whom he was alleged to have scandalously neglected. Sterne's father was a poor ensign who made an unfortunate marriage in Flanders with the daughter of a sutler: he appears to have married her because he owed money to her father. Born in 1713, Laurence spent his infancy in barracks in Ireland, and was then sent to school in Yorkshire, where he came under the protection of his father's relatives, upon whom he was dependent for the expenses of his education, his father dying penniless in 1731. During the period when Sterne was at Cambridge and for some years after his ordination as a clergyman in the Church of England, his mother lived in Ireland on her pension, supplemented by what she earned by keeping an embroidery school, and there appears to have been little contact between them. It was in 1741, when Sterne was established as a prebendary of York and married to a woman whom she believed to have money, that his mother conceived the policy of coming with her

daughter to England to live at his expense. The story of the
persecutions which he suffered over a period of years, of the
drain upon his income and his various financial anxieties, of
her unreasonableness and dishonesty and his repeated efforts
not to forget that he was a son, 'though she forgot that she
was a mother', is told in a letter by Sterne himself which
was not published until 1892. We have only his word for
its truth, but it is a circumstantial document and has the ring
of genuineness. It was written in indignation to his uncle
and old enemy, Dr. Jaques Sterne who, after playing a not
very helpful part in this affair, had caused her to be placed
in a charitable institution in York (according to some, 'the
common gaol') apparently with no other motive than the
wish to damage his nephew's reputation. Before the publication of this letter there were many, no doubt, who
believed, with Byron, that Sterne 'preferred whining over a
dead ass to relieving a living mother'. We do not know
the whole story. It seems likely that Sterne's handling of
this extremely difficult situation fell short of the heroic, but
Cross's comment that 'a man of finer grain would have
taken in his mother and sister and made the best of it', is a
lapse into insensitive moralizing. Not that moral principles
do not apply to Sterne as much as to other men, but one
of the effects of his elusive and sympathetic personality upon
us is to remind us of how little, even when we know the
'facts', we can judge any human being's response to the
strains and stresses of life.

What can be said of his character as a clergyman? It is
difficult for us to appreciate the motives with which, in this
period, men like Swift and Sterne entered the Church: they
seem to have had no special insight into their religion, no
overmastering sense of vocation. Both of these clergymen
had a distinctly secular turn of wit. Part of the answer is
that in an age when intense religious fervour was condemned
by reasonable people as 'enthusiasm', the tendency was for
clergymen to behave outwardly as men of the world, so
that it is not easy for us to tell how serious they were beneath

the surface. Sterne's sermons have little doctrinal content, and show no feeling for the supernatural values of his religion; one has the impression that he takes all this for granted. It is the human moral aspects of the Bible stories that he dwells upon, often with sensitiveness and insight, though none of his sermons rises to great heights. As for his parochial activities, from the little evidence we have it is impossible to say how diligent he was. In a letter to the Archbishop of York in 1743 replying to a *questionnaire* he makes the remarkable statement: 'I Catechise every Sunday in my Church during Lent, But explain our Religion to the Children and Servants of my Parishioners in my House every Sunday Night during Lent, from six o'clock till nine', which, according to Canon Ollard, who published the letter (in *The Times Literary Supplement*, 18 March 1926) and examined many other such returns, stands alone as an example of zeal. Sometimes the evidence points to a more easy-going attitude. Cross quotes a story to the effect that as Sterne, 'was going over the fields on a Sunday to preach at Stillington, it happened that his pointer dog sprung a covey of partridges, when he went directly home for his gun and left his flock that was waiting for him in the church in the lurch'. On the whole Cross, whose knowledge of him is unrivalled, gives him a good character for attention to his ecclesiastical duties and generosity to his curates, a class of men who in that age were not always well treated.

For nearly thirty years his associations were with York and the villages north of it: Sutton-in-the-Forest, Stillington, and finally Coxwold, the living of which he obtained in 1760. Like other parsons of his day he farmed his own land, and it is not altogether agreeable to note that he used the practice of enclosure to build up a sizeable property. That Sterne was attached in this way to his locality, with a countryman's feeling for it, is one of the things which contribute to the flavour of *Tristram Shandy*; and a love for Coxwold, his 'land of plenty' and 'delicious retreat', colours the pages of the *Journal to Eliza*, written in his last year. But in the last eight years of his life he was absent for long periods, partly because of bad health and the need to travel, partly because as a man of letters he was eagerly claimed by the society of the metropolis.

He had an unholy taste for the company of Rabelaisian wits, like John Hall-Stevenson who entertained his club of 'Demoniacs' at Skelton Castle ('Crazy Castle' as he called it), which was near enough for Sterne to pay frequent visits. In the days of his fame the freedom of his conversation gave offence to Dr. Johnson, who felt the disgrace to the cloth. *A propos* of Johnson's disapproval, it is quite likely that Sterne's anarchic wit, stimulated by an uncontrolled eagerness of temperament, often went too far, so that he gave an unjust impression of his true worth.

Sterne developed late as a literary artist. His earliest writings, as far as we know, were political articles and letters written for local newspapers during a celebrated Yorkshire election of 1741. It was as an assistant to his uncle, Jaques Sterne, who was a vigorous Whig and persecutor of Catholics and Jacobites, that he had this short spell as a political propagandist, but later he regretted it as 'dirty work', and his refusal to write any more in such a cause earned him the undying ill-will of Dr. Sterne, manifested, as we have seen, in the situation created by his mother. Apart from the occasional sermon which was printed he wrote nothing more for nearly twenty years.[1] In 1759 a local squabble about ecclesiastical preferments provoked him to compose a witty allegory in the manner of Swift entitled *A Political Romance*, later known as *The History of a Good Warm Watch-Coat*. About New Year 1760 he published the first two volumes of *Tristram Shandy*. At the age of forty-six then Sterne, hitherto quite obscure, suddenly achieved a celebrity to which there can be few parallels in literary history.

[1] Unless some literary articles in the *York Journal* of 1750–1, referred to by Dr. L. P. Curtis in his *Sterne's Politicks*, are by him, but we have no definite evidence.

Visiting London by chance a few months after *Tristram Shandy* made its *début*, he discovered that copies of it 'could not be had either for love or money'; and the news that the author was in town led to an astonishing sequence of social triumphs. Lord Rockingham, one of the great Yorkshire Whigs and a future Prime Minister, took the lead in welcoming him into the world of fashion; he made the acquaintance of the Duke of York; and he dined at Windsor, on the occasion of the installation of Prince Ferdinand of Brunswick as Knight of the Garter. Among his new friends in the world of the arts was David Garrick. Those who are not well-disposed towards Sterne may be inclined to regard this as a somewhat meretricious social success: he was an amusing companion and a fashionable novelty; but this is not the whole truth. Dr. John Hill (a dubious figure, but there is no reason to question his good faith here) wrote in a current periodical: 'Everybody is curious to see the author; and, when they see him, every body loves the man; there is a pleasantry in his conversation that always pleases; and a goodness in his heart, which adds the greater tribute of esteem.'

Further volumes of *Tristram Shandy* appeared over the next seven years, the pace of composition being greatly reduced by periods of illness and the distractions of travel abroad. On his first journey to France in 1762-4 he was given a most flattering reception into Parisian society, and became an associate of the Holbach circle. It is with his second visit to the Continent in 1765-6 that *A Sentimental Journey* appears to be mainly concerned, though some incidents from the earlier visit are incorporated; but after all it is not primarily as a factual record that we value this remarkable work of art, which was published in 1768, a few weeks before his death.

One of the more damaging of the legends which recent biographers have been able to correct concerns his death. It is not true that he died friendless and in mean lodgings. His last days were spent in comfortable apartments where he

was much visited until he was too ill—he died of pleurisy—
to receive any more, and there were friends to show him
kindness until the end. It is true, however, that he left large
debts, the sale of his works, though considerable, being insufficient to offset the expenses of foreign travel and of a
separate establishment for his wife and daughter.

II

Tristram Shandy is one of those works to which one can
return again and again with increasing satisfaction, but let
us begin by looking at it as it appears to the delighted but
baffled reader who is approaching it for the first time. His
impression is of a kind of rich chaos, an inspired disorder.
First, there is the apparent lack of progression. The reader
waits helplessly until somewhere in the third book for the
hero to be born; the christening occurs in the fourth; in
the sixth there is talk of putting him into breeches; and this,
apart from a freakish, wholly unrelated passage about his
travels in the seventh, is as far as his history is developed.
Whatever the reader is getting, it is not what the title promised: the 'Life and Opinions' of the hero. Meanwhile,
there are *digressions*. No writer, it is safe to say, ever used
the digression more often or, it would seem, more wantonly.
It would be difficult to find digressions at a steeper angle
from the main course than some of Sterne's. Yet Sterne is
completely at home and at his ease amidst this seeming
anarchy; and if the reader loses all sense of movement and
direction, something sustains him: an atmosphere so
humanly satisfying and beguiling that the author, with all his
vagaries, has him totally at his mercy.

Lying on the surface of *Tristram Shandy* are innumerable
little manifestations of Sterne's playfulness and delight in
absurdity, which serve to accentuate the impression of
artistic irresponsibility. For example, half-way through the
third book, when Mr. Shandy falls asleep as he sits in the
parlour waiting for his son to be born, and Uncle Toby

follows him, and the other characters have also been conveniently disposed of for the time being, the narrator now
decides that he has a moment or two to spare, so he writes
his Preface! When the moment arrives in the sixth book
for a picture of the Widow Wadman, the narrator abdicates
and invites the reader to supply it himself ('Sit down, Sir,
paint her to your own mind—as like your mistress as you
can—as unlike your wife as your conscience will let you—'),
leaving a blank page for the purpose. And in the last book,
when Uncle Toby is about to call on the Widow Wadman
to pay court to her, and is in fact on the threshold, the
chapter ends and the next two chapters (numbers 18 and 19)
are left blank, to be supplied out of their order a few pages
later. After the sketch of parson Yorick in the first book—
a Cervantic self-portrait, full of humour and of Sterne's
peculiar brand of pathos—a page is devoted to his tomb-
stone. At the end of the sixth book, affecting to mend his
ways and tell his story 'in a tolerable strait line', he draws a
number of irregular lines representing the tortuous paths
taken in the earlier books. And if the reader, turning over
the page from Book IV, Ch. xxiii, thinks that something
has gone wrong at the printer's, he will soon see that it is
just another of the author's jokes: there is no twenty-fourth
chapter, and there is a gap in the pagination signifying the
loss of ten pages.

But some readers will see, even on their first approach,
that there is a good deal of method in Sterne's chaos. There
is, for example, quite a good reason why the hero's birth
should be so long delayed: it is not a beginning, it is a
climax. The novel opens with his begetting, and no one
can complain of lack of promptness in the treatment of it.
In most autobiographical novels the birth and infancy of the
hero are passed over fairly quickly, the main interest being
attached to his later adventures; but Sterne's novel is
different. Its theme, to reduce it to a simple formula, is
'How the hero came into the world and how, owing to
various mishaps pre-natal and post-natal, he came to be the

unfortunate creature he is'. It is as if a modern novelist wrote a Freudian romance dealing with the decisive traumatic experiences of the central character: as in *Tristram Shandy*, it would not be necessary to trace the hero's career beyond infancy. It is part of Sterne's comic purpose that we should be somewhat befogged as to his intention, yet from the beginning there are plenty of explicit indications as to what he is doing. His technique is to dangle the point in front of the reader's nose, but also to keep him so much entertained and bewildered by other things that he will probably not see it. The present writer could not have identified the central plan of *Tristram Shandy* after the first reading, but there is no reason why an observant reader should not do so.

The first chapter begins with these words:

> I wish either my father or my mother, or indeed both of them, as they were in duty both equally bound to it, had minded what they were about when they begot me. . . .

And then follows a discourse on 'the animal spirits, as how they are transferred from father to son etc. etc.' and how much depends on their condition during this important journey; and we are told of the ill-timed question of his mother ('Pray, my dear, have you not forgot to wind up the clock?'—an example of Locke's doctrine of association of ideas, in which Sterne was much interested) which, by interrupting Mr. Shandy, 'scattered and dispersed the animal spirits, whose business it was to have escorted and gone hand in hand with the HOMUNCULUS, and conducted him safe to the place destined for his reception'. This is the first of the series of catastrophes blighting the fortunes of the infant hero.

The second arises out of a clause in Mrs. Shandy's marriage settlement, the sense of which is that if she becomes pregnant her husband undertakes to pay the expenses of her journey to and confinement in London; but if on any occasion she puts him to this expense 'upon false cries and tokens', she forfeits these rights the next time. Unluckily for the young hero a fruitless journey to London was made in the year before his birth, under peculiarly annoying circumstances for Mr. Shandy, as it was towards the end of September, 'when his wall-fruit and green-gages especially, in which he was very curious, were just ready for pulling'. The terms are enforced, it is settled that the hero shall be born in the country, and 'I was doom'd, by marriage articles, to have my nose squeez'd as flat to my face, as if the destinies had spun me without one'; but this is looking ahead.

Mr. Shandy is a man of theories, and he applies his speculative mind to the supreme parental task of ensuring that his child shall have the best start in life. One of his beliefs concerns noses; namely, that 'the excellency of the nose is in a direct arithmetical proportion to the excellency of the wearer's fancy'. The events culminating in Tristram's being brought into the world defective in this respect have therefore to be traced with some care; and, indeed, the narrator lavishes every circumstantial embellishment upon the various stages of the fatal sequence. In the first place, Mrs. Shandy is as obstinate in her own way as her husband: deprived of the best professional attention she insists on having the most primitive, the local old woman, in preference to Dr. Slop, an operator with an impressive equipment of obstetric instruments. So, by way of compromise, she gets her own way, while Dr. Slop is to sit in the parlour and drink a bottle of wine with Mr. Shandy and Uncle Toby, for which he is to receive a fee of five guineas. But as they sit there Dr. Slop is called upon, in an emergency, to intervene: the old woman has fallen on the edge of the fender and bruised her hip; and he too has suffered a somewhat Shandean misadventure, having cut his thumb while trying to sever the knots in the strings with which Obadiah, the servant at Shandy Hall, has tied up his bag of instruments. The next thing we hear of Dr. Slop, after he has been suddenly summoned imperfectly prepared to his task, is that, having applied his 'vile instruments' with disastrous effect, he is making 'a bridge for master's nose . . . with a piece of cotton and a thin piece of whalebone out of Susannah's stays'.

The dismal climax is led up to with touches of dramatic heightening. 'Truce!—truce, good Dr. Slop: stay thy obstetrick hand. . . .' Thus begins an eloquent invocation to the operator as he approaches Shandy Hall. 'Sport of small accidents, Tristram Shandy! that thou art, and ever will be!' are the bitter words provoked by Obadiah's tying of the knots.

Such is the story of the hero's birth, when the relevant details are abstracted and pieced together; but how unlike the effect of the novel, in which the fragments of the narrative have the appearance of interruptions to digressions!

One of Sterne's notable characteristics is an imaginative interest in the physiological aspects of human situations. It is no accident that the Shandean philosophy, stated on the first page of this essay, should be expressed in physiological terms. An excursion into the history of science would be necessary to explain why it was possible for Sterne and his predecessors, Rabelais and Burton, to derive so much inspiration from a subject which in modern times has not had much to give to the literary artist. The fact is that the old speculative approach to knowledge, the pre-scientific approach, offered greater opportunities to the imagination, especially in the direction of comic travesty, than the specialized experimental disciplines of later periods. Mr. Shandy with his doctrine of noses and other curious excursions into physiological theory, is a speculative philosopher of the old school. And in becoming more efficient, science has acquired a sterilized quality: the fusion of scientific ideas with a homely personal manner or a lively fancy has gone. There are certain passages in *Tristram Shandy*—for example, the last chapter of Book II, in which Mr. Shandy's mind, running on obstetrics, is excited by the advantages of the Cæsarian section (he mentions it to his wife 'merely as a matter of fact; but seeing her turn pale as ashes' drops the subject), and the later chapters of Book III, in which he goes deeply into the philosophy of noses—where his curious pedantry takes on an extraordinary richness of flavour, a flavour to which we are accustomed in Rabelais, who was immensely learned in medicine and imaginatively alive to the poetry of the bodily functions. Here, for example, is a passage dealing with the ideas of Ambrose Paroeus 'chief surgeon and nose-mender to Francis the ninth of France'. His view is

> . . . that the length and goodness of the nose was owing simply to the softness and flaccidity of the nurse's breast—as the flatness and shortness of *puisne* noses was to the firmness and elastic repulsion of the same organ of nutrition in the hale and lively— which, tho happy for the woman, was the undoing of the child, inasmuch as his nose was so snubb'd, so rebuff'd, so rebated, and so refrigerated thereby, as never to arrive *ad mensuram suam legitimam*;—but that in case of the flaccidity and softness of the nurse or mother's breast—by sinking into it, quoth Paroeus, as into so much butter, the nose is comforted, nourish'd, plump'd up, refresh'd, refocillated, and set a growing for ever.

The delight in strange words, and the play between learned and homely words, gives a piquancy to the diction reminiscent of the older writers to whom Sterne was indebted.

The atmosphere in which the drama of the hero's birth is enacted is charged, then, with obsessions: obsessions with obstetrics, with noses, and also with names. Thwarted over his son's nose Mr. Shandy turns to his theory that a name has an important positive or negative influence on its owner's destiny. If his son can be christened Trismegistus he may still enter upon life handsomely endowed. But the child has a fit, the christening has to be conducted in a hurry, and while his father, who has been roused from his bed, looks round for his breeches, the name has been irre-trievably reduced to Tristram, a name which ranks very low in Mr. Shandy's system. He is still not wholly discouraged in his attempts to apply his learning to the problems of parenthood: he composes a *Tristra-paedia*, a plan for Tristram's education, on the lines of Xenophon's *Cyropaedia*; he develops a curious theory about physical health; he discovers a short cut to knowledge based on the use of auxiliary verbs.

It is one of Sterne's structural devices to interrupt the history of the hero's birth by filling in the human background, so that the Shandy world is well peopled and familiar to us when the moment for his arrival comes. He preferred to do this in digressions, though if he had wished he could have contrived a more orthodox framework. Because the hero is not yet born these sections have the appearance of being deviations from the matter in hand and, as we have seen, it is part of Sterne's purpose that the reader should never know quite where he is. Thus several chapters in the first book are devoted to Yorick, a digression the pretext for which is rather slender: he comes in *à propos* of the old midwife to whom he used to lend his horse. And there is a sequence of chapters about Uncle Toby, with an elaborate explanation of the origin of his 'hobby-horse'. In an extremely interesting chapter (Bk. I, xxii) Sterne claims— playfully but there is serious truth in it—that his work is digressive and progressive at the same time. The digression often has a central purpose, though it also has its independent life. There are some digressions in *Tristram Shandy* for which this excuse could hardly be offered. There is something to be said for the view that freedom to digress is an artistic advantage, provided that the writer can control the tension set up between new sources of interest and the reader's anxiety to reach a promised goal; and ability to manipulate the reader in this way is certainly one of Sterne's gifts. His lyrical defence of digressions is worth remembering:

> Digressions, incontestably, are the sunshine;—they are the life, the soul of reading!—take them out of this book, for instance,— you might as well take the book along with them;—one cold

eternal winter would reign on every page of it; restore them to
the writer;—he steps forth like a bridgegroom,—bids All-hail;
brings in variety, and forbids the appetite to fail.

There is another reason for his use of digressions. One of
the features of the Shandy world is the intensity with which
the characters are absorbed in their own ideas and fantasies.
Both Mr. Shandy and Uncle Toby are, to use Sterne's
expression, 'hobby-horsical', and Sterne's greatness as an
artist is nowhere more manifest than in his ability to give
imaginative depth to their preoccupations; otherwise what
would be more boring than Mr. Shandy's theories or more
childish than Uncle Toby's toy fortifications? The two
brothers, though continually together and full of brotherly
affection, virtually inhabit different mental spheres, which
collide sometimes though they can hardly be said to meet.
Uncle Toby's 'hobby-horse' has its origin in his attempts,
while he is recovering from his wound obtained at the siege
of Namur, to explain to visitors how it all happened. The
complexity of the terrain confuses him, and the story breaks
down, so in order to clarify it he resorts to military maps
and textbooks, until his servant, Corporal Trim, has the
inspired idea of building miniature fortifications on the
bowling green, where they fight mock battles with impro-
vised field-pieces made from such materials as a melted
down pewter shaving basin and the leads from sash-
windows. As Mr. Shandy expounds his philosophical views
Uncle Toby, smoking quietly in his corner and compre-
hending little, makes remarks of engaging simplicity; but
when his brother speaks of a train of ideas, his mind turns
readily to a train of artillery, and when it is reported that
Dr. Slop is making a bridge he is very gratified, thinking
of the broken drawbridge on the bowling-green which has
given him some trouble; and the history of the drawbridge
provides us with a digression at this point. Sterne enjoyed
furnishing illustrations for Locke's theory of association of
ideas. More perhaps than any other novelist before Virginia
Woolf, who may have learnt from him, he succeeds in

capturing the atmosphere that is created when two or three people, ostensibly in conversation together, are in fact thinking their own thoughts and maintaining a rather tenuous contact with each other. 'I wish, Dr. Slop, you had seen what prodigious armies we had in Flanders', is Uncle Toby's contribution to a conversation specifically directed towards obstetrics.

Sterne is nowhere greater than in his power to convey a sense of Uncle Toby's absorption in his own private world, of its remoteness and of the completeness of the spell. It is when he takes us into that world, more than at any other time, that he shows us what he has learnt from Cervantes, to whom he continually makes affectionate references. Just as the Don's delusions are given a potency which challenges everyday reality, so that in each episode we see the events from two points of view, so Uncle Toby's curious game of make-believe is given an extraordinary inwardness. In certain passages describing his technical problems we visualize the objects as the toys they are, yet they are invested with some of the importance of the things they represent. The effect depends on the use of detail. One of Sterne's most pleasing artistic habits is that of entering delightedly into the particulars of a complicated situation: the details are felt, made real to the imagination. The following passage about the drawbridge has something of this quality:

> It turned it seems upon hinges at both ends of it, opening in the middle, one half of which turning to one side of the fosse, and the other to the other; the advantage of which was this, that by dividing the weight of the bridge into two equal portions, it impowered my uncle *Toby* to raise it up or let it down with the end of his crutch, and with one hand, which, as his garrison was weak, was as much as he could well spare—but the disadvantages of such a construction were insurmountable;——for by this means, he would say, I leave one half of my bridge in my enemy's possession——and pray of what use is the other?

Although the element of the fantastic is generously developed in the Shandy brothers, it is characteristic of Sterne's art that the better we come to know them the more they are seen to have of everyday human nature. The Shandy world is very solidly built, in spite of the magic elements in the atmosphere; whereas, for example, the best things in Dickens are entirely magical. Uncle Toby is a more real person than the great Dickens creations. He is of Shakespearian quality. Sterne can afford, in his half playful, half tender way, to give him an almost ideal charm: there are sufficient touches of plain, earthy normality to prevent the effect from being spoilt. We can believe completely in Uncle Toby, whereas it is necessary with Mr. Pickwick not to probe too far: we need to forget, for example, that he was once a business man.

A number of passages concerning Uncle Toby have always caught the fancy of Sterne's readers; for example, the too-often quoted story of the fly whom he allowed to escape: 'Go, says he, lifting up the sash, and opening his hand as he spoke, to let it escape;—go, poor devil, get thee gone, why should I hurt thee?—This world surely is wide enough to hold both thee and me.' Some of these episodes are composed rather in the manner of set pieces, an element of humorous artifice leaving the reader a certain amount of 'play' between different possible levels of emotional response. The following admirable passage occurs in the story of the poor dying soldier Le Fever upon whom Uncle Toby and Trim lavished their generous care:

——In a fortnight or three weeks, added my uncle *Toby*, smiling,—he might march.——He will never march; an' please your honour, in this world, said the corporal:——He will march; said my uncle *Toby*, rising up, from the side of the bed, with one shoe off:——An' please your honour, said the corporal, he will never march but to his grave:——He shall march, cried my uncle *Toby*, marching the foot which had a shoe on, though without advancing an inch,—he shall march to his regiment.—— He cannot stand it, said the corporal;——He shall be supported, said my uncle *Toby*;——He'll drop at last, said the corporal, and

what will become of his boy?——He shall not drop, said my
uncle *Toby*, firmly.——A-well-'o-day,—do what we can for him,
said *Trim*, maintaining his point,—the poor soul will die:——He
shall not die, by G—, cried my uncle *Toby*.

—The ACCUSING SPIRIT, which flew up to heaven's chancery
with the oath, blush'd as he gave it in;—and the RECORDING ANGEL,
as he wrote it down, dropp'd a tear upon the word, and blotted
it out for ever.

III

Sterne is a figure of European importance, but mainly as
the author of *A Sentimental Journey*. The influence of this
work was prodigious: volumes have been written on its
vogue in France, in Germany, in Italy; and countless
publications with the word 'sentimental' in the title appeared
during the generation or so after his death. It was from
outside England, from such writers as Goethe and Heine,
that the highest tributes to his genius came.

If the Victorians misread him ungenerously, disliking his
vein of sentiment, he was certainly misread in the opposite
way by some of his admirers outside England. Heine
attributes to him a kind of intensity that is not his: 'He was
the darling of the pale, tragic goddess. Once in an access of
fierce tenderness, she kissed his young heart with such
power, passion, and madness, that his heart began to bleed
and suddenly understood all the sorrows of this world, and
was filled with infinite compassion.' Those who know
Sterne will know what kind of weight—not too much nor
too little—to attach to such words as the following, which
occur in a letter: 'I told you my design in it [i.e. *A Sentimental Journey*] was to teach us to love the world and our
fellow creatures better than we do. . . .' To extract too much
moral value from Sterne's work, on the authority of
sentences such as these, may do him a disservice by pro-
voking the old objection that the sentiment he helped
to make fashionable is largely of the self-indulgent and self-
deceiving kind. The disservice lies in the fact that Sterne's
art, properly understood, forestalls this criticism. He had

more wareness of the nature of emotional self-indulgence and self-deception than most of his critics. He showed just the right degree of awareness of them in himself: to have shown more would have been a fault.

Sterne seems to have played a decisive part in helping to establish certain meanings of the word 'sentimental' in English. There has been some debate as to whether the letter of about 1739–40 to his future wife in which the word occurs, seemingly for the first time, is authentic or not. The same passage with small verbal changes is found in the *Journal to Eliza* of nearly thirty years later, which means that either Sterne touched up an old letter or his daughter Lydia, in editing the letters, fabricated one out of materials from the then unpublished *Journal*. From what we know of Lydia's editorial morals, the latter seems highly likely; and this solution becomes doubly acceptable when we consider the history of the word. The passage runs: 'I gave a thousand pensive, penetrating looks at the chair thou hadst so often graced, in those quiet and sentimental repasts.' It has been shown that this meaning of the word ('tender', 'full of emotion') does not come into vogue until the 1760's, and then mainly through the writings of Sterne himself, the earlier meanings being based on the definition of 'sentiment' as 'thought' or 'moral reflection' rather than 'feeling'. Sterne, it is suggested, was influenced by the French meaning of 'sentiment' and was responsible for attaching it to the English word 'sentimental'.

Chilly generalizations concerning Sterne's place in contemporary literary history as an instrument in the creation of a vogue, have little bearing on the essential value or interest for us of *A Sentimental Journey*. It is very much a personal achievement, a miracle not to be repeated, though there were many attempts to imitate it. It is alive and significant for us while the fashions of the period seem peculiarly dead and unreal.

To appreciate *A Sentimental Journey* we must first accept the personality of the narrator. Sterne was supremely skilled in presenting himself to the reader, a matter requiring considerable tact and the right combination of naturalness and sophistication. From the outset we see him as a somewhat slender, though engaging personality. He is sympathetically responsive, but the situations described are such as to exercise the sympathies agreeably rather than otherwise. From the *Journal to Eliza*, a more personal document, we know that he was capable of more poignant feelings, but this is not the side of his nature which he reveals here. Perhaps the most important need for us in approaching the pathetic passages is to see them in their right proportion. The most usual way of misreading them is to assume that they claim more than they do, and then to attack them for their inadequacy. It is quite permissible, quite within the range of the author's intention, that in the chapter of 'The Dead Ass', for instance, we should note his fond cherishing of the little details of the story, and see in it an element of amiable affectation:

> Everybody who stood about, heard the poor fellow with concern——La Fleur offer'd him money.——The mourner said, he did not want it—it was not the value of the ass,—but the loss of him.—The ass, he said, he was assured loved him—and upon this told them a long story of a mischance upon their passage over the Pyrenean mountains, which had separated them from each other three days; during which time the ass had sought for him as much as he had sought the ass, and that they had neither scarce eat or drank till they met.

> Thou hast one comfort, friend, said I, at least, in the loss of thy poor beast; I'm sure thou hast been a merciful master to him.——Alas! said the mourner, I thought so, when he was alive—but now that he is dead, I think otherwise.——I fear the weight of myself and my afflictions together have been too much for him—they have shortened the poor creature's days, and I fear I have them to answer for.—Shame on the world! said I to myself—Did we love each other, as this poor soul but loved his ass—'twould be something.——

In a number of incidents he allows us to see the limits or

fluctuations of his generous feelings. When the Franciscan calls on him to beg for his convent, an inexplicable perversity prompts him to give nothing, in spite of—or because of?—the altruistic after-dinner mood in which he has been interrupted. (But later they are charmingly reconciled.) And what becomes of the caged starling, the plight of which provokes him to such an elaborate outburst on liberty? In the episode of the beggars he makes admirable play with the illusions which accompany charitable giving. On the strength of eight sous, which he has arbitrarily decided is all he has for this purpose, how much moral satisfaction he extracts from the scene which follows! How he delights in the refinements of courtesy with which the beggars accept what he gives! But when he realizes that he has given away 'his last sou', and that a *pauvre honteux* must go without, 'Good God! said I—and have I not one single sou to give him—But you have a thousand! cried all the powers of nature, stirring within me. . . .'

In the following passage Sterne shows a humorous awareness of the absurdity of an infatuation, without robbing it of its charm:

> Then I will meet thee, said I, fair spirit, at Brussels—'tis only returning from Italy through Germany to Holland, by the rout of Flanders, home—'twill scarce be ten posts out of my way; but were it ten thousand! with what a moral delight will it crown my journey, in sharing in the sickening incidents of a tale of misery told to me by such a sufferer? to see her weep! and though I cannot dry up the fountain of her tears, what an exquisite sensation is there still left, in wiping them away from off the cheeks of the first and fairest of women, as I'm sitting with my handkerchief in my hand in silence the whole night beside her.

It is surprising that he has not been more valued for these corrective effects. There are two kinds of sophistication in him which our age might well find enjoyable: his recognition of foibles and vanities in the sphere of the affections and sympathies, and his uninhibited expression of the latter, notwithstanding this recognition.

How are we to take those episodes dealing with encounters with women? They are, as sexual adventures, rather slender: that he was not more passionate is, for some readers, a point against him. For other readers, the point against him is the philandering in itself. For others again it is his lingering over the details, his cherishing of each vibration. If we like Sterne, what will please us in these incidents is their fragrance, which this lingering over the details never spoils, and his gaiety of conscience. The fact is that for him such experiences are good. A point which needs to be made is that Sterne really believes in 'virtue', though he cannot resist a woman's charm, and the sweetness of the episodes in question lies in the amount he gets out of them without actual transgression. In 'The Conquest' he conveys admirably a fact of experience which is normal enough; namely, that it can be pleasant to feel desire and also pleasant not to give full rein to it. After he has refrained from laying hands on the *fille de chambre*, and has raised her up by the hand, led her out of the room, locked the door and put the key in his pocket, *then*, 'the victory being quite decisive', he kisses her on the cheek and takes her safe to the gate of the hotel. In the episode of the girl in the bookshop there is as much subtle suspense and intimacy of atmosphere as if it had been the beginning of an amorous intrigue:

> We stood still at the corner of the Rue de Nevers whilst this pass'd—We then stopp'd a moment whilst she disposed of her *Egarements de Coeur*, etc. more commodiously than carrying them in her hand—they were two volumes; so I held the second for her, whilst she put the first into her pocket; and then she held her pocket, and I put in the other after it.
>
> 'Tis sweet to feel by what fine-spun threads our affections are drawn together.
>
> We set off afresh, and as she took her third step, the girl put her hand within my arm—I was just bidding her—but she did it of herself with that undeliberating simplicity, which shew'd it was out of her head that she had never seen me before. For my part, I felt the conviction of consanguinity so strongly, that I

could not help turning half round to look in her face, and see if I could trace out any thing in it of a family likeness—Tut! said I, are we not all relations?

When we arrived at the turning up of the Rue de Gueneguault, I stopp'd to bid her adieu for good and all: the girl would thank me again for my company and kindess—She bid me adieu twice—I repeated it as often; and so cordial was the parting between us, that had it happen'd anywhere else, I'm not sure but I should have sign'd it with a kiss of charity, as warm and holy as an apostle.

But in Paris, as none kiss each other but the men—I did, what amounted to the same thing—

—I bid God bless her.

The delicacy of his narrative technique in episodes like these is one of his important contributions to the art of the novel. And with what piquancy and wit he describes the participants! Here is his description of Madame de L——, the object of his fantasies in the early chapters of the book:

When the heart flies out before the understanding, it saves the judgment a world of pains—I was certain she was of a better order of beings—however, I thought no more of her, but went on and wrote my preface.

The impression returned, upon my encounter with her in the street; a guarded frankness with which she gave me her hand, shewed, I thought, her good education and her good sense; and as I led her on, I felt a pleasurable ductility about her, which spread a calmness over all my spirits—

Good God! how a man might lead such a creature as this round the world with him! . . .

When we had got to the door of the Remise, she withdrew her hand from across her forehead . . . it was a face of about six and twenty—of a clear transparent brown, simply set off without rouge or powder—it was not critically handsome, but there was that in it, which in the frame of mind I was in, attached me more to it—it was interesting; I fancied it wore the characters of a widow'd look, and in that state of its declension, which had passed the two first paroxysms of sorrow, and was quietly beginning to reconcile itself to its loss. . . .

All these effects in Sterne may be examined in terms of technique in the handling of prose. Of all English novelists none had greater virtuosity in this respect. Sir Herbert Read, in an excellent introduction to *A Sentimental Journey*, has called attention to his range of styles, from the easy conversational manner of the opening chapter to the studied beauty of his description of 'The Captive', in the starling episode. It would be possible, taking his work as a whole, to identify a considerable number of ways in which prose is exploited to give to particular types of passage their essential flavour and tone. He is highly individual, but with all his idiosyncrasies he has the great eighteenth-century virtues: order, proportion, and a regard for fineness of surface.

While *A Sentimental Journey* has the virtues of a novel, it is, with much allowance made for embellishment, an account of incidents which really occurred and people whom he really met. Monsieur Dessein, the Calais hotel-keeper, made his fortune out of his appearance in Sterne's masterpiece; the Franciscan turns up some years later in Mrs. Piozzi's *Journey Through France*; rumour was active concerning the identity of Madame de L——. An absorbing interest in people, in all kinds of people, high and low, gives that quality to his work which, in the man himself, was perhaps the chief reason why he was so much sought after. That it should have been composed when he was in desperate health shows that, whatever his philosophy of life amounted to, it was not altogether a vain one.

LAURENCE STERNE

Select Bibliography

BIBLIOGRAPHIES

Catalogue of Sterne's Library. Edited by C. Whibley. New York: Wells, 1930.
A facsimile of the rare sale catalogue of Sterne's books.

Laurence Sterne: A List of Critical Studies Published from 1896 to 1946. Edited by F. Cordasco. Brooklyn: Long Island University Press, 1948.

YOKLAVICH, J. M. "Notes on the Early Editions of 'Tristram Shandy,' " *PMLA*, Vol. LXIII (1948).

OATES, J. C. T. "On Collecting Sterne," *The Book Collector*, Vol. I (1952).
There is a detailed bibliography in Wilbur L. Cross, *The Life and Times of Laurence Sterne*—see below.

COLLECTED EDITIONS

The Sermons of Mr. Yorick. 7 vols. London: Dodsley and others, 1760–1769.
There were various eighteenth-century reprints.

Works. 6 vols. Philadelphia: Humphreys, 1774.
The first American edition. There were numerous eighteenth-century collected editions.

Works. Edited by George Saintsbury. 6 vols. London: Dent, 1894.

Works. Edited by Wilbur L. Cross. 12 vols. New York: Taylor, 1904.

Works. Shakespeare Head Edition. 7 vols. Oxford: Blackwell, 1926-1927.

SELECTION

Sterne. Edited by Douglas Grant. Cambridge: Harvard University Press, 1951.
Includes *Memoirs, Tristram Shandy, Sentimental Journey*, sermons, and letters.

LETTERS

Letters From Yorick to Eliza. London, 1775.

Letters to His Friends. London, 1775.

Letters of the Late Mr. Laurence Sterne. 3 vols. London, 1775.

Seven Letters. Edited by W. D. Cooper. London, 1844.

Letters. Selected and edited by R. B. Johnson. New York: Dodd, Mead, 1927.

Letters. Edited by L. P. Curtis. Oxford: Clarendon Press, 1935.
The standard edition.

SEPARATE WORKS

Note. Dates of original publication are given. Modern editions and paperbacks are also recorded here.

The Case of Elijah. York, 1747. *Sermon*.

The Abuses of Conscience. York, 1750. *Sermon*.

A Political Romance. London, 1759. *Polemics*.
Later known as *The History of a Good Warm Watch Coat*.

The Life and Opinions of Tristram Shandy. 9 vols. London, 1759–1767. *Novel*.

Everyman's Library; The World's Classics; Macdonald's Illustrated Classics; Dolphin Paperback; edited by S. Holt Monk (Rinehart Edition); Modern Library.

A Sentimental Journey Through France and Italy. 2 vols. London, 1768. *Travel*.

Introduction by G. Saintsbury (Everyman's Library); introduction by V. Woolf (The World's Classics); introduction by H. Read (London: Scholartis Press, 1929).

The Second Journal to Eliza. Edited by M. R. B. Shaw. London: Bell, 1929.
The authenticity of this work is very doubtful.

BIOGRAPHICAL AND CRITICAL STUDIES

FERRIAR, J. *Illustrations of Sterne*. Manchester, 1798.

COLERIDGE, S. T. *Literary Remains*. Vol. I. London: Pickering, 1836.

FITZGERALD, P. *The Life of Laurence Sterne*. 2 vols. London: Chapman and Hall, 1864.

STAPFER, P. *Laurence Sterne, Sa Personne et ses Ouvrages*. Paris: Thorin, 1870.

TRAILL, H. D. *Sterne*. English Men of Letters. London: Macmillan, 1882.

BAGEHOT, W. *Estimations in Criticism*. Edited by C. Lennox. 2 vols. London: Melrose, 1909.
Includes a study "Sterne and Thackeray."

CROSS, WILBUR L. *The Life and Times of Laurence Sterne*. New York: Macmillan, 1909; 2nd ed. with important additions (New Haven: Yale University Press, 1925); further revisions (New Haven: Yale University Press, 1929).
This is the standard work on Sterne.

SICHEL, W. *Sterne*. Philadelphia: Lippincott, 1910.

WRIGHT, ARNOLD, AND W. L. SCLATER. *Sterne's Eliza*. London: Heinemann, 1922.

DEFROE, A. *Sterne and His Novels in the Light of Modern Psychology*. Groningen: Noordhoff, 1925.
Despite its shortcomings, an interesting analysis.

CURTIS, L. P. *The Politicks of Laurence Sterne*. London: Oxford University Press, 1929.

READ, HERBERT. *The Sense of Glory*. Cambridge: University Press, 1929.
Includes a study of Sterne.

WOOLF, VIRGINIA. "The Sentimental Journey," in *The Second Common Reader*. New York: Harcourt, Brace, 1932.
Other essays by Virginia Woolf about Sterne appear in her *The Moment* (1947) and *Granite and Rainbow* (1958).

LAIRD, JOHN. *Philosophical Incursions into English Literature*. Cambridge: University Press, 1946.
Includes "Shandean Philosophy."

DILWORTH, E. N. *The Unsentimental Journey of Laurence Sterne*. New York: King's Crown Press, 1948.
A study of Sterne's attitude to sentimentalism.

HAMMOND, L. H. *Sterne's "Sermons of Mr. Yorick."* New Haven: Yale University Press, 1948.

ERÄMETSÄ, E. *A Study of the Word "Sentimental."* Helsinki: Finnish Academy of Sciences, 1951.
Relevant to passages on page 100 of this essay.

TRAUGOTT, JOHN. *Tristram Shandy's World: Sterne's Philosophical Rhetoric*. Berkeley: University of California Press, 1954.

HOWES, ALAN B. *Yorick and the Critics: Sterne's Reputation in England 1760–1868*. New Haven: Yale University Press, 1958.

FLUCHÈRE, HENRI. *Laurence Sterne, de l'Homme à l'Oeuvre*. Bibliothèque des Idées. Paris: Gallimard, 1961.

TOBIAS SMOLLETT

by Laurence Brander

TOBIAS SMOLLETT
From a painting about 1770 by an unknown Italian artist,
in the National Portrait Gallery, London

TOBIAS SMOLLETT was born in 1721 in Scotland; he died in 1771 in Italy.

TOBIAS SMOLLETT

I

THE portrait of Smollett in the National Portrait Gallery suggests a man of intelligence, energy, and determination. The long self-portrait in his *Travels through France and Italy* suggests the same virtues, along with a sharp sort of humour not far removed from the spleen. The two went together in eighteenth century authorship with very enjoyable results.

In his last novel, *Humphry Clinker*, Smollett introduces a picture of his earlier life in Chelsea, and in this picture there is a self-portrait:

> By all accounts, Smollett is not without weakness and caprice, but he is certainly good humoured and civilized : nor do I find that there is anything overbearing, cruel or implacable in his disposition.

Autobiography is a dangerous weakness; everything that is put in or left out can be used against the writer. Weakness and caprice are the common human lot and only a strong man will make a claim against them. Good humour and being civilized are virtues which every eighteenth-century man would wish to claim; but why should Smollett, a writer who balanced his words, claim that he was not overbearing, cruel, or implacable unless the charge had been made against him with some force?

The charges which can be brought against him as author of *Roderick Random* and *Peregrine Pickle* are those which will be brought to-day against the author of picaresque novels, and will include cruelty. The other epithets could have been earned by his journalism when he was a dominating figure in literary London from 1750 to 1762. He was possibly the outstanding figure in literary London between the death of Pope and the great reign of Johnson.

In the picture already referred to Smollett says:

> I saw none of the usual signs of authorship, either in the house or in the landlord, who is one of those few writers of the age

that stand upon their own foundation, without patronage and above dependence.

But for Johnson's famous letter to Lord Chesterfield ('Is not a Patron, my Lord, one who looks with unconcern on a man struggling for life in the water, and, when he has reached ground, encumbers him with help?') this might have become the common quotation in literary histories to mark a change over from patronage to another economic system of authorship.

Smollett ran a literary factory in Chelsea while Johnson was running one in Pump Court, off the Strand, for his dictionary. Both claimed independence from patronage: neither stressed their dependence upon other writers who were capable of hard work and incapable of dealing to advantage with the publishers. Independence is a claim that does not bear sifting. Both were good business men, working with energy and enterprise for the general good of authorship.

Smollett was an innovator in literary kinds and methods. He was the first to publish a long historical work in weekly parts at a popular price; he was the first to publish a full-length novel as a serial in a weekly journal. He raised critical standards by editing for seven years an independent journal in the days when most critical reviews were subsidized advertisement sheets for the publishers.

Smollett is known to-day as the author of three novels and a book of travels, but his life story is one of immense literary activity and energy. Placed against that forgotten work, these four books seem almost by-products; which is the way great imaginative books are sometimes written. Smollett was an entrepreneur in literature, a doctor by profession, who burst upon literary society with a successful novel at the age of twenty-seven, repeated his success three years later, and gave up his first profession to devote his extraordinary energy to literature. He wanted to organize it, to found an Academy, to improve the conditions of authorship and to improve criticism so that writing would improve and fulfil its function in society.

He failed. The memory of his efforts has almost disappeared and all the volume of writing, in journalism, criticism, compilation, and history which he did himself and inspired in others has been forgotten.

He was a Scotsman, born of good family in Dumbartonshire in 1721. He studied medicine in Glasgow and very soon, in the familiar Scots way, he went to London. He joined the Navy as a surgeon, and went on the Carthegena Expedition in 1741. This was part of the maritime war with Spain begun in 1739 about South American trade. The Navy had not been on active service for a long time and the Expedition was badly organized and ended in disaster. Smollett wrote a pamphlet on the subject, one of his first attacks on muddle-headed stupidity. His experiences gave him copy for his novels, so that it might almost be said that the best things that came out of the Expedition were the sailors in *Roderick Random* and *Peregrine Pickle* and the satirical treatment of it in *Roderick Random*.

Smollett found a wife in Jamaica and settled in London in 1744 to practise medicine from a house in Downing Street. He was living near by in Mayfair in 1746 when the news of the battle of Culloden broke on London and the citizens went Mafeking-mad with relief after being hysterical with fear of invasion by the Scots and their Stuart claimant to the throne. Two or three years later, he settled in Chelsea, where he worked as a writer until his health broke in 1762. Chelsea was then a small town and the road to the City of Westminster was sometimes the hunting ground of footpads and highwaymen. The soft air of Chelsea seems to have been as congenial to authorship then as it is now.

From 1763 to 1765 Smollett lived in France and Italy, spending most of the time at Nice. He returned to England and spent much of his time travelling; and when he was not travelling he lived in Bath, at that time a focus for English society. In 1768 he returned to northern Italy, for so many

years an author's annexe for England, and settled down in
a house near Leghorn, where he died in 1771. He was buried
in the English cemetery there, an old, neglected place now;
how different from the English cemetery in Lisbon, bright
with flowers, where Fielding lies.

II

The forgotten mass of his work may be considered first,
as it is relevant to the study of the four books which are
read to-day.

Smollett seems to have begun his career as a journalist by
working on the *Monthly Review* for Ralph Griffiths, the
bookseller in St. Paul's Churchyard. It was after some
experience of this kind of work that he wrote:

> The miserable author must perform his daily task, in spite of
> cramp, colick, vapours, or vertigo ; in spite of head-ach,
> heart-ach, and *Minerva's* frowns ; other wise he will lose his
> character and livelihood, like a taylor who disappoints his
> customers in a birth-day suit.

In 1755 he broke away and projected a new journal which
he called the *Criticial Review*. From 1756 until his breakdown in 1762 he controlled its policy and no doubt used his
factory for producing copy.

The proposals for this *Review*, which he called *Proposals
for publishing Monthly, The Progress or Annals of Literature
and the Liberal Arts*, appeared in the last days of 1755. They
indicate the position which this young man hoped to fill
in the London literary world of the mid-eighteenth century.

> This Work will not be patched up by obscure Hackney
> Writers, accidentally enlisted in the Service of an undistinguish-
> ing Bookseller, [so much for Master Ralph Griffiths and his
> ilk] but executed by a Set of Gentlemen whose Characters
> and Capacities have been universally approved and acknow-
> ledged by the Public : Gentlemen, who have long observed
> with Indignation the Productions of Genius and Dullness ;

Wit and Impertinence ; Learning and Ignorance, confounded
in the Chaos of Publication ; applauded without Taste and
condemned without Distinction ; and who have seen the noble
Art of Criticism reduced to a contemptible Manufacture
subservient to the most sordid Views of Avarice and Interest,
and carried on by wretched Hirelings, without Talent, Candour,
Spirit or Circumspection.[1]

The tone of these *Proposals* indicates the fervour of
Smollett's campaigning in early maturity for a better literary
London. His scheme for an Academy of Letters never got
nearer to realization than in these Proposals, and in the
conduct of the *Critical Review*.

His immense energies were absorbed at the same time in
his *Complete History of England, Deduced from the Descent of
Julius Caesar to the Treaty of Aix La Chapelle, 1748. Containing the Transactions of One Thousand Eight Hundred and
Three Years.* He worked on it from 1755 to 1757 and it
was published in four handsome quarto volumes in 1757 and
1758. His contract to James Rivington and James Fletcher
seems to have been for the first three quartos which were
published together in April 1757, bringing the history
up to the end of the reign of William and Mary. The
fourth volume appeared eight months later. The idea
appears to have come from the booksellers who got it from
Hume's *History*, which began publication in 1754 and was
completed in 1761. Hume published in Edinburgh and
the London booksellers probably hired Smollett so that they
could exploit the idea for London sales. It was certainly
not a Tory answer to Hume's sceptical and Whig approach,
for Smollett began with Whig leanings and only later on,
as he worked, did he discover a Tory outlook.

He revised the whole thing in 1758 for publication in
weekly parts at sixpence, showing good publishing sense in
doing so and being the first writer in London who published
a history in a popular format. He told Dr. Moore that
orders rose to 10,000 and there is a story that his publishers

[1] *Public Advertiser*, 30 December 1755.

addressed an early part to every parish clerk in the country, enclosing half a crown and asking them to push sales by letting people see it.

In 1760 Smollett began publishing a *Continuation* to his *History*, planning forty sixpenny parts covering the twelve years from the end of 1748. This contemporary survey was admirably written with an urbanity very different from the scratching and biting attacks so common in his journalism. The *Continuation* made amends for all that, and he took the opportunity of the aloof approach of the historian to write of his contemporaries with detachment, good sense, and often with magnificent compliment. This *Continuation* was used during the next eighty years at the end of Hume's *History*, often with title pages which suggested that Smollett sat down in the first place to continue Hume.

The labour of the *History* undermined his health. He wrote it down in Chelsea, it is said in fourteen months, working with absurd concentration, refusing himself to callers, worried by debt and by duns and with it all laying himself open to the tuberculosis which then first attacked him and eventually killed him.

During this intensive historical writing he at least allowed himself the luxury of other kinds of writing, for in 1756 he wrote *The Reprisal*, a brief play for performance after the main piece which was produced by Garrick in 1757 at the Theatre Royal in Drury Lane. This was generous of Garrick and when Smollett revised *Peregrine Pickle* in 1758 the satire on Garrick's acting was removed.

In the beginning of 1760 he launched *The British Magazine*, which ran till 1767. Much work for it had been prepared prudently before the journal was launched, and it is distinguished by carrying some of the finest essays of Oliver Goldsmith. It was here that *Sir Launcelot Greaves* appeared in serial form.

Meanwhile, also, he continued to be the life and soul of the *Critical Review*. On one occasion he cast doubts upon the courage of an Admiral, who dealt with him in peremptory

sailor fashion and in November 1760 Smollett disappeared
for eleven weeks into the Marshalsea prison. Prison conditions were made easy for him and apparently his writing
went on without interruption.

He was engaged furthermore all this time in translation
work and in the oversight of the immense compilations
his literary factory produced.

Finally and unfortunately he was persuaded to edit the
Briton, a political weekly which appeared from May 1762
to February 1763 in defence of Bute's ministry. Here he
walked into real trouble, for his chief opponent was his
old friend John Wilkes, who was so much the master of
Smollett at this kind of work that he scored off him with
the greatest of ease. The *Briton* formed a focus for attacks
on the Scots, at that time peculiarly unpopular in London,
and Wilkes at the head of the local brigade of political
journalists smiled and smote in the *North Briton*. This was
bad enough for anyone as sensitive as Smollett. What was
worse was the corroding effect of an excursion into politics
on an eager and spirited worker for the betterment of
society. It ended as it was bound to end, in bitter dis-
illusionment.

By the summer of 1762 Smollett was seriously ill and
eventually in the summer of 1763 he cut himself away from
all his burdens and went to France and Italy. This record
of his writing up to his illness marks his extraordinary
energy. He always worked well and sometimes with
genius. All the time he was urged on by the belief that if
only man would think and organize, society would progress
to happiness. Especially, he was haunted by a belief that
the world of letters would exert its proper influence if it
were organized.

All this journalism died with him. It was popular at the
time, apart from the political stuff, but it has never been
read since and his great efforts for improving literature and
the arts, whether by academies or by improving periodical

criticism, have left no apparent result.   None of it, except the *History* and its *Continuation*, has ever been reprinted.

The Adventures of an Atom (1769) must have been written during his last stay in Britain, some time after the period of his great activity just described.   It is a vindictive satire of current affairs and public characters from 1754 to the date of publication and it is Smollett's last fling at the politicians before he left them for ever.   It could hardly be further away from the urbanity of his *Continuation*.   The fiction under which the satire is maintained is that an atom moves from Japan to the brain of one Nathaniel Peacock, and dictates what he must write of its ' Japonese ' adventures. Any doubts about the true subject matter are dispelled in an early paragraph, which is an unmistakable portrait of the English people :

> The Japonese value themselves much upon their constitution, and are very clamorous about the words liberty and property ; yet, in fact, the only liberty they enjoy is to get drunk when they please, to revile the government, and quarrel with one another. With respect to their property, they are the tamest animals in the world ; and, if properly managed, undergo, without wincing, such impositions as no other nation in the world would bear.

Soon there follows the exceptionally disgusting descriptions which make all devout critics ignore the book or deny that Smollett wrote it.   Yet immediately afterwards the prose pictures of ministers are so good that they recall Dryden's verse pictures. Pages of explosive virulence follow, directed against military and naval commanders, every statesman in the country and especially Chatham.   The common people, the political mob, are almost the most loathly of all.   Indeed the text of the book might be Swift's ' I cannot but conclude the Bulk of your Natives, to be the most pernicious Race of little odious Vermin that Nature ever suffered to crawl upon the Surface of the Earth '.

The Swiftian rancorous spleen is in Smollett's performance, but nothing of Swift's peculiar greatness, nothing of the ease, almost the magnanimity, of Swift's condemnation of the human race. Smollett has a smaller man's concentrated virulence and eventually a certain weariness with the whole performance overtakes the reader. Perhaps Smollett did not write it. He never admitted authorship : and friendly critics have always either denied his authorship or left the question open. Yet, so many of these characters are so well done, and so many of the sentences are quotable and memorable ; and the main unpleasant theme, the sycophancy of public life, is so much Smollett's lifelong special hate that it is difficult to suggest he had nothing to do with it. If Smollett did not write it, what other perverted genius did?

III

We come now to the three novels and the book of travels which are generally read to-day. Smollett was third of the four writers who set the English novel on its way. *Roderick Random* was published in 1748, in the same year as Richardson's *Clarissa*, and within the decade which saw the great beginnings. *Pamela* (1740) begat Fielding's *Joseph Andrews* (1742) and *Tom Jones* followed in 1749. In 1751 came *Peregrine Pickle*, with its obvious inspiration to Sterne's *Tristram Shandy* (1760–7). *Humphry Clinker* (1771) completed the series which set the novel on its way.

According to the picaresque convention, Smollett claims a satirical and reforming intention in the preface to *Roderick Random* :

> Of all kinds of satire, there is none so entertaining and universally improving, as that which is introduced, as it were, occasionally.

The reader is a sensible and sober citizen, who must have some excuse for enjoying a book in which the morals are those of a thieves' kitchen. The same convention is used in *Gil Blas*, which Smollett translated and published in 1749.

It had been used, with much greater comic skill, by Fielding
in the opening of *Jonathan Wild* (1743).   Smollett blurs his
comedy by breaking seriously into satire, especially in his
descriptions of life in the Navy.   Indeed, he seems to have
chosen picaresque, with the familiar gallery of odd characters, usually criminal types, strung together in a series of
episodes, because he had a grudge against society.   He had
tried verse as a vehicle for his satire, and had failed ; he
would now try prose.

Roderick Random is the orphaned, unwanted grandson
of a severe old Scots magistrate, exposed by his grandfather's
known neglect to the malice of the community.   His principal enemies are the schoolmaster and the young heir.   It
is not long before a *deus ex machina* appears in the form of
a sailor uncle, and for the first time a British tar appears
in the English novel :

> He was a strongly built man, somewhat bandy-legged, with
> a neck like that of a bull, and a face which (you might easily
> perceive) had withstood the most obstinate assaults of the
> weather.   His dress consisted of a soldier's coat, altered for
> him by the ship's tailor, a striped flannel jacket, a pair of red
> breeches japanned with pitch, clean grey worsted stockings,
> large silver buckles that covered three-fourths of his shoes,
> a silver laced hat whose crown overlooked the brim about an
> inch and a half, a black bob wig in buckle, a check shirt, a silk
> hankerchief, a hanger with a brass handle girded on his thigh
> by a tarnished laced belt, and a good oak plant under his arm.

What a subject for the publisher of illustrated editions—
' red breeches japanned with pitch ' !   This excellent officer
proceeds at once to discomfit the heir, flog the schoolmaster
and interview grandfather.   His speech is as good as his
costume and for the first time we hear the salt spray accents
in English fiction :

> Your servant, your servant.   What cheer, father?   What
> cheer?   I suppose you don't know me ; mayhap you don't.
> My name is Tom Bowling, and this here boy : you look as
> if you did not know him neither ; 'tis like you mayn't.   He's
> new rigg'd i' faith ; his cloth don't shake in the wind so much

as it wont to do.   'Tis my nephew, d'ye see, Roderick Random, your own flesh and blood, old gentleman. 'Don't lay astern you dog !' pulling me forward.

'The Navy's here' once again and for a while all goes well with Roderick Random.   But the sailor returns to sea, leaving the youngster settled with a Mr. Potion, the apothecary in a neighbouring town, who turns him away when misfortune overtakes Tom Bowling.   Mr. Crab, the surgeon, takes him in, because it will harm Potion, his rival. His school friends and relations melt away, and incident after incident reflects the cynicism of the young novelist.

His virtues as a writer are already apparent in these early chapters.   He has the golden pen, the style which wraps one round.   Characters and incidents follow one another in teeming plenty and only a strong stomach is required to carry the reader forward, ready to follow Roderick Random anywhere.   And indeed, there is some exertion in travelling, or there would be but for the easy vehicle of this fine eighteenth-century prose.   Character after character appears, sketched with the clear crudeness of an old woodcut, or designed as it were for the caricaturists like Rowlandson who were to spring from this English society as naturally as Smollett himself.   Crab, the surgeon, is a good example of this prodigality for here he is, and he lasts only for a part of a chapter:

> This member of the faculty was aged fifty, about five feet high, and ten round the belly ; his face was capacious as a full moon, and much of the complexion of a mulberry ; his nose resembled a powder-horn, was swelled to an enormous size, and studded all over with carbuncles ; and his little grey eyes reflected the rays in such an oblique manner, that while he looked a person full in the face, one would have imagined he was admiring the buckle of his shoe.

Excellent average eighteenth century, matched later only by Dickens, who profited by study of Smollett.

There is no resisting these characters and these incidents unless we are built so that they are both too harsh and too gross for us. We may find it difficult to realize, partly because of this harshness, partly because of the remoteness of eighteenth-century society, that for Smollett and his reader this was a picture of contemporary life in which many known characters were recognizable.

The hero eventually joins the Navy as a doctor, which gives Smollett his opportunity to describe with minuteness and trenchancy the inefficient methods of recruitment at that time. Eventually he puts to sea, and the first of the long series of stories of the Silent Service begins.

It is at once apparent that there was much besides perfection to keep the Navy silent in those days, for Smollett is concerned to describe the evil conditions on ships. (' A man had better go to prison than go to sea', said Dr. Johnson) and to expose the incompetent management of the Carthegina Expedition. This celebration of the character of the Navy and its sailors is the best part of the book. The ocean and the winds of the world form the background to many English stories of the little societies of men on ships ; and the special atmosphere of these seafaring societies against their elemental background is caught in *Roderick Random* for the first time. While Smollett was writing, the British Empire was in the making and the two great influences of vast land and sea spaces, so different from island atmosphere, were beginning their work on the English character.

The great ocean influence is nowhere consciously stated by Smollett as it is by Conrad, but it is inherent in his subject.

The indignation of the young doctor at conditions at sea finds trenchant expression :

> I assisted Thomson in making up his prescriptions : but when I followed him with the medicines into the sick berth or hospital, and observed the situation of the patients, I was much less surprised that people should die on board, than that any sick person should recover. Here I saw about fifty miserable distempered wretches, suspended in rows so huddled upon one

another that not more than fourteen inches space was allotted
for each with his bed and bedding ; and deprived of the light
of the day as well as of fresh air ; breathed nothing but a
noisome atmosphere of the morbid steams exhaling from their
own excrements and diseased bodies, devoured with vermin
that hatched in the filth that surrounded them, and destitute
of every convenience necessary for people in that helpless
condition

Smollett's descriptive comments on the Carthegina Expedition are of a kind to which we have grown accustomed
after two world wars.   Smollett's treatment is classical,
for no expedition could exceed the Chartheginan in the
stupidity of its conduct and no writer could surpass the
happy gusto of this young genius.

Chapter 33 is a *locus classicus* for all war commentators.
Smollett makes short shift with the tactics of the commanders, writing for example of a particularly atrocious tactical
blunder :

> This piece of conduct afforded matter of speculation to all
> the wits either in the Army or Navy, who were at last fain to
> acknowledge it a stroke of policy above their comprehension.

He deals with the medical and quarter-master's arrange-
ments with equal delight.   Yet it is not for these things that
Roderick Random is celebrated as the first of our naval
novels, but for the descriptions of sailors, of storms at sea,
and of the never-failing wonder at what common men can
endure against the elements and their leaders.

Eventually the hero returns to England and lands not in
any normal way, for this is a picaresque novel, but by ship-
wreck and in fighting with his shipmates on the shore.

The normal adventures of a picaresque hero then follow.
He becomes manservant in a local family and falls in love
with the young lady of the house, the fair Narcissa.   He
goes abroad and serves as a common soldier in the French
Army, which gives an opportunity for discussing the battle

of Dettingen.[1]   His old friend Strap reappears to rescue
him.   These sudden reappearances of favourite characters
to prove the truth of the adapted saying, ' cast your bread
upon the waters and it will come back buttered after many
days ' is a piece of machinery frequently used.   Thomson,
who threw himself overboard in despair, survived to feed
and outfit the hero and set him on his way in Jamaica.   In
the end his father comes to life again and restores the family
fortunes so that the hero, now an undoubted gentleman,
rent-roll and all, can marry Narcissa.   It is all engagingly
simple, and supplies the only continuity the plot boasts.

The picaresque atmosphere is oppressive, principally
because of the moral concepts the hero follows.   He must
never work honestly for his living.   He may fight duels,
gamble, try to marry for money and accept whatever he
needs from his equals and agents.   He may not be cowardly
or mean, rather he must be foolishly brave and foolishly
generous.   His enemies may outwit him, but in the end
picaresque justice demands that the hero or his good fortune
overcomes them.   It is never suggested that he is an enemy
of society or that society has a case against him.   The quarrels
are all with individuals and there is no hint that behind it
all there may be a social structure which is damaged by his
conduct.   The sense of social structure only comes at the
end, for he must be admitted again to honourable place (that
is, position and money) so that he may marry and live
happily ever afterwards.

The next novel, *Peregrine Pickle*, is equally offensive to us
in these ways.   It is rescued from being utterly sordid by
the great character, Commodore Hawser Trunnion and
his shipmates, retired from the sea and settled on land as
part of English village society.   The hero rises out of English
village society, which is to say average English society in

[1] Though nothing he has to say of it matches this note to his satire,
Advice (1746) : ' This line relates to the behaviour of a General on a
certain occasion : who discovered an extreme passion for the cool shade
during the heat of the day : the Hanoverian General, in the battle of
Dettingen.'

those days. This brings the novel nearer to Fielding, who had an unfailing sense of social structure. Smollett usually preferred the shifting scene of London, where many societies have their own laws and customs.

Trunnion is so much more real than any character in the first novel that it may be described as a rapid development since *Peregrine Pickle* was first published in 1751, only three years later. It was heavily revised by Smollett and re-published in 1758, about fifty pages shorter, the slanderous sketches of contemporaries being removed. It is invariably the revised edition which is reprinted to-day.

Commodore Trunnion was as lost ashore as a whale. He garrisoned himself with old shipmates against all the perils of the land, and chief amongst these were women and lawyers. When everyone, including the garrison, leagued against him to marry him, he was lost and in a brief passage of high comedy, which is one of the most delicious things in the eighteenth-century novel, he makes his proposals of matrimony.

On the wedding day the groom set out on horseback ' at the head of all his male attendants, whom he had rigged with the white shirts and black caps formerly belonging to his barge's crew '. Yet he did not arrive in time, indeed the bridal party

> waited a whole half hour for the commodore, at whose slow-ness they began to be under some apprehension, and accordingly dismissed a servant to quicken his pace. The valet, having rode something more than a mile, espied the whole troop disposed in a long file, crossing the road obliquely, and headed by the bridegroom and his friend Hatchway, who, finding himself hindered by a hedge from proceeding farther in the same direction, fired a pistol, and stood over to the other side, making an obtuse angle with the line of his former course ; and the rest of the squadron followed his example, keeping always in the rear of each other like a flight of wild geese.
>
> Surprised at this strange method of journeying, the messenger came up, and told the commodore that his lady and her company

expected him in the church, where they had tarried a considerable time, and were beginning to be very uneasy at his delay ; and therefore desired he would proceed with more expedition. To this message Mr. Trunnion replied, ' Hark ye, brother, don't you see we make all possible speed? Go back, and tell those who sent you, that the wind has shifted since we weighed anchor, and that we are obliged to make very short trips in tacking, by reason of the narrowness of the channel ; and that, as we lie within six points of the wind, they must make some allowance for variation and leeway'. ' Lord, sir ! ' said the valet, ' what occasion have you to go zig-zag in that manner? Do but clap spurs to your horses, and ride straight forward, and I'll engage you shall be at the church porch in less than a quarter of an hour.' 'What ! right in the wind's eye,' answered the commander ; ' ahey ! brother, where did you learn your navigation? Hawser Trunnion is not to be taught at this time of day how to lie his course, or keep his own reckoning. And as for you, brother, you best know the trim of your own frigate.'

Apart from the Trunnion group, which was so finely conceived that it inspired Sterne's Uncle Toby and his friends in *Tristram Shandy*, the old coarseness and sordid atmosphere remain and these qualities haunted Smollett in his next two novels and only left him in his great final masterpiece. There was some quirk in his nature which drove him, as through his early books it drove George Orwell later, to expend his genius on description of filth. And there is no doubt that Smollett's medical training gave added force to this idiosyncracy.

Peregrine Pickle is essentially similar in kind to *Roderick Random*, but Commodore Trunnion with his counterpart Lieutenant Hatchway and his retinue of sailors make it the greater book. This is not only by their own value as characters but because they acquire their full value by contrast with Peregrine's household and society in the village inn, which introduce, if only for a short space in the book's great length, good normal contemporary eighteenth-century English country life.   The poorest part of the book is the long interruption ' The Memoirs of a Lady of Quality ' which Smollett's publishing sense of good-selling exclusive scandal made him include and certainly gave the book notoriety when it was published, but remains now a very deadly dull appendage.

His next novel, *Ferdinand Count Fathom* (1753) is plain picaresque and shows how poor the kind can be when no sailors or other bright characters come to relieve the tedium of repeated similar incident. *Sir Launcelot Greaves* (1760–1) was a contemporary English *Dox Quixote* and the reader may get some amusement from it if he is good enough to ignore the fact that the hero would have been arrested after the first adventure.

Two books, the best Smollett wrote, and heartily to be commended to any reader, remain for consideration. In the *Travels through France and Italy* Smollett is an early example of the personal travel writer, conforming to Mr. Norman Douglas's specification that it is the mind of the traveller that matters. Some of his comments are famous ; his suggestion that a Corniche road would pay dividends ; his forecast of trouble for France as soon as there was a weak monarch ; his remark on the natural use of the Borghese as a gallery ; his recommendation that the Roman Campania be drained and cultivated—adopted as it were only yesterday ; the commonplace that the entry to London from the south is a disgrace to any metropolis—which is being worked on to-day but largely remains for a better to-morrow.

This is probably the first English book of travel which is interesting because it reflects the state of a man's mind ; the first of a kind in which English writers have displayed a special aptitude. The state of Smollett's mind when he set out is described by himself :

> Traduced by malice, persecuted by faction, abandoned by false patrons, and overwhelmed by the sense of a domestic calamity, which it was not in the power of fortune to repair.

Echoes there of the *Briton*, of his service to Lord Bute, who discarded him ; of Wilkes, who laid about him ; and of the loss of his fifteen-year-old daughter, from which he and his wife never recovered. The *Travels* were written as he went along in the form of letters addressed to the circle of Scots doctors in London who were his close friends, and we may pleasantly presume that these physicians had a talk amongst themselves before he left. They knew how ill Smollett was, and they knew that part of the cure would be for him to escape from the exertions of daily writing ; but they also knew that it would be unwise for him to stop suddenly and altogether ; so they proposed the letters or encouraged him when he made the suggestion, explaining how useful a record of inns, prices, and methods of transport would be to them if they wished to make the Tour them-selves. So Smollett tells them exactly what he thought of the inns between London and Dover, and all the inn-keepers he suffered from in France and Italy. He offered detailed and apparently sound advice on transport, and he told them of the cost of living everywhere.

He discussed water supplies and food as one doctor to others. More personally he describes the state of his health, and in one letter (the only one which opens ' Dear Doctor ') he describes his exchange of letters with a French specialist on tuberculosis.

Two letters, the seventh and fifteenth, are addressed to the wife of one of the doctors (was it Mrs. Moore?). The first was the famous attack on the French and the second was an attack on duelling, a subject chosen carefully for his correspondent after her reproof about his harsh judgement of the French, to whom he makes amends in the opening of the later letter.

In the other thirty-nine letters one of the finest living English journalists addresses an audience fit and few over a period of two years. The first is dated Boulogne, June 1763, and he is delighted to have left England. In the last, Boulogne, June 1765, he is greatly recovered, in body and spirit and records his pleasure at seeing again ' the white cliffs of Dover '.

He is an honest travel critic. 'I assure you, upon my word and honour, I have described nothing but what actually fell under my own observation.' Moreover, he says what he thought, and not what he should have thought. He was disappointed in Paris and Rome, and what honest traveller is not at first disappointed in places he has read about all his life and then first sees?

The less-known places are different. The shock of surprise can be pure pleasure, as in Smollett's first sight of the Maison Carrée at Nîmes :

> The proportions of the building are so happily united, as to give it an air of majesty and grandeur, which the most indifferent spectator cannot behold without emotion. A man need not be a connoisseur in architecture, to enjoy these beauties. They are indeed so exquisite that you may return to them every day with a fresh appetite for seven years together. . . . Without all doubt it is ravishingly beautiful. The whole world cannot parallel it ; and I am astonished to see it standing entire, like the effects of enchantment, after such a succession of ages, every one more barbarous than another.

That was written in Montpellier in November 1763. By September Boulogne had become too cold and Smollett heard that Nice was an ideal wintering place. He reached it in December and stayed there until the autumn of the following year, when he went to Italy. The letters from Nice, as from Boulogne, are full of people and places and all the other things which would delight his correspondents.

In Italy he spent most of his time in Florence and Rome and his letters are full of art criticism and a vast deal of Latin learning. His taste in painting was very different from ours, and he enjoyed sculpture more, lingering with an anatomist's pleasure over the sculpture in the Pincio. But he always had space for what was present and lively. The English lived then in and around the Piazza D'Espagna,[1] and he remarks :

> When you arrive at Rome, you receive cards from all your

[1] Where Keats and Severn had rooms sixty years later.

country-folks in that city : they expect to have the visit returned next day : when they give orders not to be at home ; and you never speak a word to one another in the sequel. This is a refinement in hospitality and politeness, which the English have invented by the strength of their own genius, without any assistance either from France, Italy or Lapland.

All through the *Travels* Smollett is at his best in the quick sketches of inns and inn-keepers, postilions, and travellers. The worst of them, and so the best to read about, were between Nice and Genoa. At Noli :

> We ascended by a dark, narrow, steep stair, into a kind of public room, with a long table and benches, so dirty and miserable, that it would disgrace the worst hedge ale-house in England. . . . At length the landlord arrived, and gave us to understand, that he could accommodate us with chambers. In that where I lay, there was just room enough for two beds, without curtains or bedstead, an old rotten table covered with dried figs, and a couple of crazy chairs. The walls had once been white-washed : but were now hung with cobwebs, and speckled with dirt of all sorts, and I believe the brick-floor had not been swept for half a century.

A night or two later :

> At the post-house in Lerici, the accommodation is intolerable. We were almost poisoned at supper. I found the place where I was to lie so close and confined, that I could not breathe in it, and lay all night in an outward room upon four chairs, with a leather portmanteau for my pillow.

What happened on these occasions to poor Mrs. Smollett we are never told. No fellow traveller could be more dim. Only once, when Smollett flew into a rage at an inn outside Florence and insisted on defying inn-keeper and coachman and walking through the night into the city, do we catch a glimpse of the poor lady :

> Behold us then in this expedition ; myself wrapped up in a very heavy greatcoat, and my cane in my hand. I did not imagine I could have walked a couple of miles in this equipage, had my life been depending ; my wife a delicate creature, who

had scarce ever walked a mile in her life ; and the ragamuffin before us with our boxes under his arm. The night was dark and wet ; the road slippery and dirty ; not a soul was seen, nor a sound was heard : all was silent, dreary, and horrible. I laid my account with a violent fit of illness from the cold I should infallibly catch, if I escaped assassination, the fears of which were the more troublesome as I had no weapon to defend our lives. While I laboured under the weight of my greatcoat which made the streams of sweat flow down my face and shoulders, I was plunging in the mud, up to the mid-leg at every step, and at the same time obliged to support my wife, who wept in silence, half dead with terror and fatigue.

Recollecting all these unequal struggles with rapacious inn-keepers and cheating postilions as he wrote in the tranquillity of Nice, Smollett is obliged at last to admit that they were not worth the few sixpences he saved.

The *Travels* is a fine book, worthy to stand beside Fielding's *Voyage to Lisbon* (1754), Sterne's *Sentimental Journey* (1768) and Johnson's *Journey to the Hebrides* (1775). Sterne met Smollett in Rome and in Turin and each time found him fulminating. He caricatured him as Smelfungus in the *Sentimental Journey* and lays his finger on Smollett's weakness for being miserable and angry. ' "I'll tell it", cried Smelfungus, " to the world." " You had better tell it ", I said, " to your physician." ' Good common sense, and Smollett recognized it in the last letters, when he was a much fitter man. He was moving pleasantly towards the self-portrait in *Humphry Clinker*, ' good humoured and civilized '.

There was something in Smollett's nature that irritated him excessively when he saw the cruelty and craft of man to man. Examples occur again and again in the early novels like raw gashes in the comic body of his work. They are more controlled in the *Travels* because his greater power permitted restraint. In his last novel, the masterpiece, they are woven into the comic structure, becoming part of the caricature figures. *Humphry Clinker* is composed with the serenity of mastery. Smollett had at last come to terms with life and expressed his views through the medium of a style that adorns a century of great prose stylists.

Humphry Clinker was published in June 1771, three months before his death. Once again he uses the letter form, and once again, as always, his characters travel. Once again he innovates, for the letters are not written by one character but five, a device only used once before and in verse, in Anstey's *New Bath Guide* (1766). The joy of this method is that episodes are seen through different eyes and the characters comment on one another as their story proceeds.

The chief character and the chief letter writer is Matthew Bramble, who is very largely an ideal self-portrait of Smollett. He is Smollett's vehicle for comment on life, he is the kindly agent for good, exerting to that end his wealth, his experience, and his position. His nephew, Jeremy Melford, writes the other long letters, and these carry the main burden of the story. The other three writers are ladies, as the great novel readers were the ladies and Smollett made few business errors.[1]

Miss Tabitha Bramble was Matthew's sister, a sourly ageing spinster in search of a husband. Lydia Melford was the heroine, and a very pleasant one. Win Jenkins was the comic maid whose letters, happily brief, enjoy like her mistress's the old comedy confusion of misspellings and malapropisms.

For the three ladies there are three men, Lieutenant Lismahago, one of the great English comic characters, Mr. Wilson, and Humphry Clinker himself. Lismahago makes a true comedy entrance :

> A tall, meagre figure, answering, with his horse, the description of Don Quixote mounted on Rozinante, appeared in the

[1] 'Tim had made shift to live many years by writing novels, at the rate of five pounds a volume ; but that branch of business is now engrossed by female authors, who publish merely for the propagation of virtue, with so much ease and spirit, and delicacy, and knowledge of the human heart, and all in the serene tranquillity of high life, that the reader is not only enchanted by their genius, but reformed by their morality.'— (*Humphry Clinker*).

twilight at the inn door, while my aunt and Liddy stood at a window in the dining-room. He wore a coat, the cloth of which had once been scarlet, trimmed with Brandenburgs, now totally deprived of their metal; and he had holster-caps and housing of the same stuff and same antiquity. Perceiving ladies at the window above, he endeavoured to dismount with the most graceful air he could assume; but the ostler neglecting to hold the stirrup when he wheeled off his right foot, and stood with his whole weight on the other, the girth unfortunately gave way, the saddle turned, down came the cavalier to the ground, and his hat and periwig falling off, displayed a head-piece of various colours, patched and plastered in a woeful condition. . . .

He would have measured above six feet in height had he stood upright; but he stooped very much; was very narrow in the shoulders, and very thick in the calves of his legs, which were cased in black spatterdashes. As for his thighs, they were long and slender, like those of a grasshopper; his face was at least half a yard in length, brown and shrivelled, with projecting cheek-bones, little grey eyes on the greenish hue, a large hook-nose, a pointed chin, a mouth from ear to ear, very ill furnished with teeth, and a high, narrow forehead, well furrowed with wrinkles. His horse was exactly in the style of its rider; a resurrection of dry bones which (as we afterwards learned) he valued exceedingly, as the only present he had ever received in his life.

Each of the five writers has a brief letter at the beginning which swiftly gives their character, so that in a very few pages all the characters are outlined firmly and a love story is indicated which will no doubt end happily but could hardly be in a more unfortunate state than when the story opens.

The action is mainly in Bath, London, Edinburgh, the Scottish Highlands, and on the Welsh border, and on all the roads between these places. The story stands completely still (it is simple enough and waits easily) during the Scottish tour. It is generally agreed that Smollett wrote a good part of the book during his last stay in Britain, for many of the descriptions of places and of society have the air of recent observation. Matthew Bramble's letter from Bath on 23 April has comments on town planning and architecture which were surely written on the spot; and much of the Scottish tour bears the marks of recent observation. The final shape, colour, and atmosphere were probably applied in Italy.

He still does without a plot of any consequence, and relies instead upon letting his characters travel and meet odd people and run into odd incidents on the road. The difference is that he is no longer writing picaresque. He is celebrating the England and the Scotland in which he has spent his life. He writes with an exile's love of his native land and people and this changes and deepens the quality of his writing. *Humphry Clinker* is one of the great pictures of eighteenth-century England, a picture of England at a great moment in her history, a record of a society which was launching out to change the appearance of half the world.

It stands with *Tom Jones* and *Tristram Shandy*, *The Decline and Fall* and the *Speeches On Conciliation*, *The Lives of the Poets* and *The Vicar of Wakefield*; and the reader who has enjoyed them will enjoy *Humphry Clinker* the better. For these great pieces are nearly two hundred years away now and though the English character has not changed much and not advanced on the ideals held then, English society has changed a great deal. They were written before the Industrial Revolution, the longest and most vile of those comparatively bloodless Revolutions that threaten the English spirit. The spirit of that former age can be recaptured only by considerable reading of what was thought and well expressed.

In an extraordinary passage towards the end of *Humphry Clinker*, Smollett draws a picture of the ideal eighteenth-century society, which like *The Deserted Village* and other pieces, records what might have been as if in foreknowledge of the dark revolution that was on the way. Matthew Bramble, in his letters about Dennison and Baynard, expresses the eighteenth-century nostalgia for the ideal country life, the craving for a well-ordered society based on the perennial round of toil on the good earth. Our eighteenth century never failed to have a strong feeling of the need for good society in living the good life and Smollett is at pains to show that the good and socially desirable life can be lived in the country. Your town author, then as now, has no doubts on the matter.

There is no warmer passage in the book than the letter from Matthew Bramble, to his friend Baynard, recommending the ideal life of the country gentleman. So the Scots' exile in Italy, who had nearly killed himself in his overworked life in London, comes at the end to subscribe to the country ideals of eighteenth-century England.

Smollett was one of the four writers who set the English novel on its way and his greatness is to be measured partly by the extent to which he inspired later novelists. Hawser Trunnion and his garrison inspired Sterne's Uncle Toby and Corporal Trim. Scott and Dickens acknowledge their debt. There are many others ; and in general it may be claimed that all the novels about the sea and the English sailor descend from him.

The student's assessment must be that Smollett stands high among the four. The ordinary reader to-day may take a different view. If Fielding and Sterne were altogether abstracted from the furniture of our minds, the loss would be more noticeable than if Smollett were taken away. Yet the loss would be great enough if Morgan and Martin Ratlin and Commodore Trunnion were missing ; and the loss of Matthew Bramble and Lieutenant Lismahago would be greater still.

In assessing Smollett we think in terms of the characters he created, so we look back for comparisons over just two centuries of character drawing in the novel. It is a large gallery, with many styles. The reader of George Eliot's *Middlemarch* catches the surprise of style difference when suddenly, during the rich enjoyment of the character play in that novel, someone mentions Smollett. George Eliot uses the rich potentiality of the novel for showing the

principal characters developing and modifying by their
contact with their environment and more fixed, older
characters.   The novel moves with the pace of life itself ;
the slow years and the sudden crises.   At the moment of
one of these crises in the life of Dorothea, the heroine, that
stupid and sympathetic character, Mr. Brooke, recommends
the reading of Smollett to her sick, pedantic husband :

> . . . get Dorothea to read you light things, Smollett, *Roderick
> Random, Humphry Clinker* : they are a little broad, but she may
> read anything now she's married, you know. I remember
> they made me laugh uncommonly—there's a droll bit about a
> postilion's breeches. We have no such humour now.

Indeed they hadn't.   That simple, early novel sort of
humour after the quiet, pointed wit of George Eliot is like
the guffawing of boys at play.   There was an equal difference in the character drawing.   Smollett never develops
characters.   He creates them brilliantly, as we have seen,
in a few sentences, then sets them moving and talking among
the other characters.   He makes them and he is responsible
for bringing them together so that the maximum amount of
fun is extracted from them.   They are comedy characters,
created and used in Ben Jonson's way, by interplay without
development.

In the guise of Matthew Bramble, Smollett carries his
responsibility one stage further.   Matthew Bramble concerns himself to help other people and the novel becomes a
much more serious consideration of life than his earlier ones.
It faces the simple and recurring human problem of living
with other people and living one's own life at the same time.
Therefore we still turn to Smollett, as we turn to Fielding
and Sterne, for that humorous comment on life which is
one of the great legacies from our indispensable eighteenth
century.

We may regard Smollett as a good European.   His
novels derive from Cervantes and Le Sage whose works he
translated.   When he set his factory to translate Voltaire
he added the notes on the prose works himself.   More

generally, like so many of his English contemporaries, he derives from the literature of Rome. His comedy is like Latin comedy. His ideals—of gravity, of humanity, of disciplined industry and the proper organization of all human affairs—are Roman ideals. And his final belief, that man is at his best and happiest in a country society, reminds us of Cicero's words on the farmer's life : ' nothing better, nothing more attractive, nothing more suitable for a free man '.

TOBIAS SMOLLETT

Select Bibliography

BIBLIOGRAPHIES

CORDASCO, F. *Smollett Criticism 1925–1945*. Brooklyn: Long Island University Press, 1947.

———. *Smollett Criticism 1770–1924*. Brooklyn: Long Island University Press, 1948.

There is a bibliography by J. P. Anderson in David Hannay, *Smollett*—see below, and a bibliography of collected editions in F. Cordasco, *Letters*—see below.

COLLECTED EDITIONS

Plays and Poems. With Memoirs of the Life and Writings of the Author. London: Evans, 1777.

Miscellaneous Works. Containing Novels, Poems, Plays, and Travels. 6 vols. Edinburgh: Ramsay, 1790.

Miscellaneous Works. With Memoirs of his Life and Writings by R. Anderson. 6 vols. Edinburgh: Mundell, 1796.
Reprinted, with enlarged Memoir, 1800.

Works. With Memoirs of his Life by J. Moore. 8 vols. London: Law, 1797.
New edition edited by J. P. Browne (London: Bickers, 1872).

Novels. With a Memoir by Sir Walter Scott. Ballantyne's Novelist's Library. 2 vols. Edinburgh: Ballantyne, 1821.

Miscellaneous Works. With a Memoir of the Author by T. Roscoe. London: Bohn, 1841.
Frequently reprinted throughout the nineteenth century.

Works. Selected and edited by D. Herbert. Edinburgh: Nimmo, 1870.
Frequently reprinted before the end of the nineteenth century.

Works. Edited by George Saintsbury. 12 vols. Philadelphia: Lippincott, 1895.
> Reprinted 1899, 1902, etc., and by the Navarre Society, 1925.

Works. Edited by W. E. Henley and T. Seccombe. 12 vols. Westminster: Constable, 1899–1901.

Works. Edited by G. H. Maynardier. 12 vols. New York: Sproul, 1902.

Novels. Shakespeare Head Edition. 11 vols. Oxford: Blackwell, 1925–1926.

LETTERS

The Letters of Tobias Smollett. Edited by Edward S. Noyes. Cambridge: Harvard University Press, 1926.

Letters of Tobias George Smollett. A Supplement to the Noyes Collection. Edited by F. Cordasco. Madrid: Avelino Ortega, 1950.
> Five of these letters are not authentic. See *Philological Quarterly*, Vol. XXXI (1952), 299–300.

SEPARATE WORKS

> Note. Dates of original London editions are given. Modern editions and paperbacks are also recorded here.

Advice: A Satire, 1746. *Verse*.

Reproof: A Satire, 1747. *Verse*.
> Reprinted with *Advice*, 1748.

The Adventures of Roderick Random. 2 vols. 1748. *Novel*.
> The World's Classics; Dolphin Paperback; Everyman's Library; Premier Paperback.

The Regicide: Or, James the First of Scotland, A Tragedy, 1749. *Drama*.

The Adventures of Peregrine Pickle. 4 vols. 1751. *Novel*.
> Revised by the author, 1758.
> Everyman's Library.

A Faithful Narrative of the Base and Inhuman Arts That Were Lately Practised Upon the Brain of Habbakkuk Hilding. By Drawcansir Alexander. 1752. *Essay*.

An Essay on the External Use of Water, with Particular Remarks Upon the Mineral Waters at Bath, 1752. *Essay*.
> Edited by C. E. Jones (Baltimore: Johns Hopkins Press, 1935).

The Adventures of Ferdinand Count Fathom. 2 vols. 1753. *Novel*.

A Compendium of Authentic and Entertaining Voyages. 7 vols.
> Edited by Smollett. 1756. *Anthology*.

The Reprisal: Or, The Tars of Old England, a Comedy, 1757. *Drama.*

A Complete History of England from the Descent of Julius Caesar to the Treaty of Aix La Chappelle. 4 vols. 1757–58; 2nd ed., 11 vols., 1758–1760. *History.*

The Adventures of Sir Launcelot Greaves. 2 vols. 1762. *Novel.*
    First published in *The British Magazine,* Vols. I, II (1760-1761).

A Continuation of the Complete History. 4 vols. 1760–61. *History.*
    A fifth volume was added in 1765. See L. M. Knapp, "The Publication of Smollett's *Complete History* and *Continuation,*" *The Library,* Vol. XVI (1935).

The Present State of all Nations. 8 vols. Edited by Smollett. 1768-1769. *Anthology.*

Travels Through France and Italy. 2 vols. 1766. *Travel.*
    Reprinted with Smollett's corrections in The World's Classics; introduction by Sir Osbert Sitwell (The Chiltern Library).

The History and Adventures of an Atom. 2 vols. 1769. *Satire.*
    Some copies are dated 1749.

The Expedition of Humphry Clinker. 3 vols. 1771. *Novel.*
    Vol. I of the first edition is misdated 1671.
    Everyman's Library; The World's Classics; Rinehart Paperback; Modern Library; Nelson Classics; Signet Paperback.

Ode to Independence. Glasgow, 1773. *Verse.*

PERIODICALS EDITED BY SMOLLETT

The Critical Review: Or Annals of Literature, 1756–1790.
    Smollett was editor-in-chief from 1756 to 1763, and an occasional contributor thereafter.

The British Magazine: Or Monthly Repository, 1760–1767.

The Briton, 1762–63.
    Smollett also contributed to *The Monthly Review.* See B. C. Nangle, *The Monthly Review, Indexes of Contributors and Articles.* Oxford: Clarendon Press, 1934.

TRANSLATIONS BY SMOLLETT

The Adventures of Gil Blas. By A. R. Le Sage. 4 vols. 1749.

Don Quixote. By M. de Cervantes Saavedra. 2 vols. 1755.

The Works of Voltaire. 36 vols. 1761–1769. Three volumes were added later. Smollett had only a small part in the translations, but wrote

all the historical and critical notes for the volumes completed by
May 1763.

The Adventures of Telemachus. By F. de Salignac de la Mothe Fénelon
2 vols. 1776.

BIOGRAPHICAL AND CRITICAL STUDIES

ANDERSON, R. *Life with Critical Observations on His Works.* Edinburgh:
Stirling, 1820.
In Volume I of Smollett's *Miscellaneous Works,* 6 vols.—see above.
The best of many memoirs by R. Anderson.

IRVING, JOSEPH. *Some Account of the Family of Smollett of Bonhill: with a
Series of Letters by T. Smollett hitherto unpublished.* Dumbarton: Priv.
Ptd., 1859.
Reprinted in Joseph Irving, *The Book of Dumbartonshire.* 3 vols.
(Edinburgh: Johnston, 1879).

HANNAY, DAVID. *Life of Tobias George Smollett.* London: Scott, 1887.

SMEATON, W. H. O. *Tobias Smollett.* Famous Scots Series. New York:
Scribner's, 1897.

BUCK, HOWARD S. *A Study in Smollett, Chiefly "Peregrine Pickle."*
New Haven: Yale University Press, 1925.
Includes a scrutiny of the edition of 1758.

WHITRIDGE, ARNOLD. *Tobias Smollett. A Study of His Miscellaneous
Works.* New York: Columbia University, 1925.

MELVILLE, LEWIS. *Life and Letters of Tobias Smollett, 1721–1771.* London:
Faber and Gwyer, 1926.
Lewis Melville is the pseudonym of L. S. Benjamin.

BUCK, HOWARD S. *Smollett as Poet.* New Haven: Yale University Press,
1927.

JOLIAT, E. *Smollett et la France.* Paris: Champion, 1935.
Contains a bibliography of translations of Smollett's works.

MARTZ, L. L. *The Later Career of Tobias Smollett.* New Haven: Yale
University Press, 1942.

JONES, CLAUDE E. *Smollett Studies.* Berkeley: University of California
Press, 1942.
Contains a bibliography.

KAHRL, G. M. *Tobias Smollett. Traveler-Novelist.* Chicago: University
of Chicago Press, 1945.

BOEGE, F. W. *Smollett's Reputation as a Novelist*. Princeton: Princeton University Press, 1947.
Contains a bibliography.

KNAPP, L. M. *Tobias Smollett, Doctor of Men and Manners*. Princeton: Princeton University Press, 1949.
The fullest modern study.

GOLDBERG, M. A. *Smollett and the Scottish School: Studies in Eighteenth-Century Thought*. Albuquerque: University of New Mexico Press, 1959.

THE EIGHTEENTH-CENTURY NOVEL

Select General Bibliography

HAZLITT, WILLIAM. *Lectures on the English Comic Writers*. London: Taylor, 1819.
The World's Classics, 1920.

THACKERAY, WILLIAM MAKEPEACE. *The English Humorists of the Eighteenth Century*. London: Smith, Elder, 1852.
Everyman's Library, 1912.

SCOTT, SIR WALTER. *Lives of Eminent Novelists and Dramatists*. London: Warne, 1887.

DOBSON, AUSTIN. *Eighteenth Century Vignettes*. 3 vols. New York: Dodd, Mead, 1892–1896.
The World's Classics, 1923.

RALEIGH, SIR WALTER. *The English Novel*. London: Murray, 1894.

STEPHEN, LESLIE. *Hours in a Library*. New York: Putnam, 1894.

PRIESTLY, J. B. *The English Comic Characters*. New York: Dodd, Mead, 1925.

SLAGLE, KENNETH C. *The English Country Squire as Depicted in English Prose Fiction 1740–1800*. Philadelphia: University of Pennsylvania, 1938.

The Age of Johnson: Essays Presented to Chauncey Brewster Tinker. New Haven: Yale University Press, 1949.

CORDASCO, F. *The 18th Century Novel: A Handlist of General Histories and Articles of the Last Twenty-Five Years*. Brooklyn: Long Island University Press, 1950.

KETTLE, ARNOLD. *An Introduction to the English Novel*. London: Hutchinson, 1951.

McKILLOP, A. D. *The Early Masters of English Fiction*. Lawrence: University of Kansas Press, 1956.

WATT, IAN. *The Rise of the Novel: Studies in Defoe, Richardson and Fielding*. Berkeley: University of California Press, 1957.

FORD, BORIS, ed. *From Dryden to Johnson*. The Pelican Guide to English Literature Vol. IV. Baltimore: Penguin Books, 1957.

TAVE, STUART M. *The Amiable Humorist: A Study in the Comic Theory and Criticism of the Eighteenth and Early Nineteenth Centuries*. Chicago: University of Chicago Press, 1960.

MAYO, R. D. *The English Novel in the Magazines, 1740–1815*. Evanston: Northwestern University Press, 1962.

McBURNEY, W. H., ed. *Four before Richardson*. Lincoln: University of Nebraska Press, 1963.

Further studies and reference works are listed in: *The Cambridge Bibliography of English Literature*, 4 vols. (1941) and *Supplement* (1957); the Annual Bibliographies published in *PMLA* by the Modern Language Association of America; *The Year's Work in English Studies*, a survey of important critical books and articles, published annually for the English Association by Oxford University Press; the *Annual Bibliography of English Language and Literature*, an extensive listing of critical books and articles, published for the Modern Humanities Research Association by Cambridge University Press; Louis A. Landa, and others, eds., *English Literature, 1660–1800: A Bibliography of Modern Studies, 1926–1950*, 2 vols. (Princeton University Press, 1950–1952); G. J. Kolb, and C. A. Zimansky, eds., *English Literature, 1660–1800: A Bibliography of Modern Studies, 1951–1960*, 2 vols. (Princeton University Press, 1962); "English Literature, 1660–1800: A Current Bibliography," published annually in *Philological Quarterly* (1961–in progress); and I. F. Bell and D. Baird, eds., *The English Novel 1578–1956: A Checklist of Twentieth Century Criticisms* (Denver: Swallow, 1959).